Irons By Irons

By David Irons

Dave Irons
5/27/96

TABLE OF CONTENTS

ACKNOWLEDGMENTS AND COMMENTS OF INTEREST

Collecting irons for over 30 years was truly interesting and fun, but nothing compares to what I've seen in the last six months while compiling material for this book. Collector friends that were asked to contribute to this book provided me with a large selection of rare and unusual (some almost unbelievable) irons. Picture groupings came in the mail from all over the U.S. and England. Receiving a group of pictures was like a six year old opening presents on Christmas morning. Some irons were novel and different, while others were more like a decorator's dream. Many were "one-of-a-kind" that I had never seen before. It was then that I finally realized that no one will ever see the last different or rare iron. I thank all those collector friends who offered irons and provided their own complimentary pictures and descriptions. You guys added the ice cream to the cake. I only wish I could have asked more collectors to contribute. Each of you undoubtedly has one or more of those unusual and rare pieces.

To my wife and family, thanks is only a small return for all those pushes and encouragements to get started. But that wasn't all by a long shot - how about the editing, long photo sessions and all of the behind-the-scenes work. And don't forget all the time devoted to buying and cleaning and the effort to display the collection over the years. And I don't want to forget my Pop, John Irons, who went on buying trips, traded and provided the initial challenge to feed my desire to collect. In retrospect, you know what? Everyone was glad to help and I believe they enjoyed it all.

Special thanks to Marty and Buck Carson and Anne and Paul Holtzman for allowing us to intrude on your homes to borrow and photograph irons. The collections of the Carsons and the Holtzmans provided many iron pictures for this book.

Also, special thanks goes to long-time friends and collector/dealers Diana and Dick Taylor who not only encouraged me to write this book, but also provided valuable technical information and knowledge on irons and equally important English teacher assistance. Thanks Diana and Dick, for the great help.

Thanks, also, to Harry Rinker Jr. for the wonderful color and black and white photographs. Harry, the details on the iron pictures are just great.

Also, special thanks to Harry Rinker Sr. of Rinker Enterprises for the needed advice in planning the book, and to Dana Morykan for her expertise in its preparation.

And finally, I would be remiss if I failed to mention all those antique dealers who found irons and saved them under the table for me. Thanks and keep up the good work! I'm not quitting yet!

TRENDS IN COLLECTING IRONS

During the 1960s iron collecting was considered to be somewhat odd. Few individuals collected irons and dealers were glad to unload their stash on any crazy collector. Prices of irons in the '60s were generally 25¢ to $1.50. Rare irons were priced under $10.00. Children's swan irons sold for about $1.00. My first German Dragon iron was $4.50. Most antique shops had 10 - 30 irons to select from, and flea markets contained a bonanza of ironing items.

The '70s brought a general increase in the prices of irons, typical of antiques in general at that time but, for the most part, iron collecting was still an off-beat antiques area. Irons of all types and rarity were readily available at flea markets, shops and antiques shows. In general, *good irons* sold for $100 or less by the late 1970s. New books by A. H. Glissman, E. Berney and J. Politzer, as well as specialized clubs and meetings, gave collectors valuable pictorial and reference information to formulate new collecting interests and wants. For the first time, iron collectors and dealers were now more knowledgeable and more willing to pay for the better irons.

The '80s, unlike the previous 20 years, were much like a runaway train in terms of frenzied selling and spiralling prices of irons. Prices for irons and antiques "went through the roof." Iron prices broke the $100, $200 and $300 levels early in the decade, and by the end of the '80s, a $500 price was not uncommon for a very rare iron. Interest in irons also blossomed. Prior to the '80s, my wife often commented that "no one ever looks at our displayed collection of irons," and neither of us thought that irons would appreciate to the extent that they did. In the '80s, for the first time, availability of irons was starting to be a problem. This happened because may more individuals were involved with collecting and many more new individuals were also dealing in ironing items. By the end of the '80s and early '90s, iron collectors had difficulty finding a *good iron* on a buying trip. More recently, collectors complain about not buying anything of significant value at shows and markets to add to their collections.

ARE IRONS A GOOD INVESTMENT?

I can easily state that prices of irons are now at an all-time high. Even though prices of antiques in general have softened in many areas in the '90s, iron prices have remained high. More collectors are hunting and wanting irons, and the availability has decreased markedly at flea markets, antiques shops and shows. It is my belief that irons will continue to appreciate in value and will be a good investment that can be enjoyed. I would stress, however, if resale or investment is a motivation to collect, that the buyer collect the better quality or the rarest irons that can be found at market prices. Historically, it is known that in most fields of antiques, the "better" and "best" in a category are more readily salable and, hence, will be in more demand when sold relative to the economic conditions at that time.

SUGGESTIONS ON CLEANING AND PRESERVING IRONS

Caring for one's irons is an important consideration for any collector, and each collector will have an individual approach. Most irons found by a collector at shops and flea markets will have surface rust and some pitting. Brass will no doubt be tarnished, and original surfaces will likely be dirty and dull if not over-painted. I offer the following as suggestions regarding the cleaning and care of irons:

Comments on cleaning

(1) Light surface rust can be removed readily with fine steel wool (#0 or finer grade). Buffing with a motorized wire wheel is another very good method to remove rust and maintain surface patina. Sand blasting is a harsh treatment that can change surface patina and is not recommended. Fine emery paper can be used, but I prefer steel wool and buffing.

(2) Heavy rust with surface pitting is a major problem. Wire wheel buffing is often the best approach followed by mild sanding with emery paper. Pitting cannot be removed unless the area is sanded away or filled with a metallic liquid metal compound and then smoothed. Oxalic acid and naval jelly can be used on heavy rust, but I prefer buffing.

(3) Dirt and oil on iron or original painted surfaces can be removed by mineral spirits or mild soap/water using fine steel wool or a rag. I suggest starting with the least abrasive method first (soap/water and a rag) and if this approach is not successful, proceed to a more abrasive and/or stronger detergent. Liquid soaps with ammonia can actually remove paint; hence, concentrated soaps should be used carefully.

(4) Tarnished brass can be cleaned by liquid brass/metal polishes with fine steel wool. Buffing compounds along with a fabric buffing wheel are also effective. If a brass surface is too black, I would clean it to a gold surface color, but not a highly polished brass. A fine brass wire wheel can be used to remove a black surface more quickly than liquid polishes. Lacquering a polished brass surface will maintain a shine that survives for years. I prefer a slightly polished surface and no lacquering.

(5) Non-original paint on iron can be removed by any number of paint removers. I prefer a semi-paste remover (Zip Strip since it has less odor) followed by fine steel wool to clean the surface.

(6) Paint applied over original paint can be removed to save the original but restoration is not easy and requires much time. Such restoration should generally be handled by an expert if the value of the iron warrants restoration costs.

Protecting the surface of cleaned irons

(1) A light rust inhibiting oil (WD-40 or other) can be applied to the cleaned iron surfaces with a rag with good results.

(2) Waxing of the surfaces and handles with a paste wax can be used to give more shine, but this approach is not long lasting at preventing rust.

(3) A surface coating of a mix of boiled linseed oil and turpentine (1 to 1 mix by volume) will minimize rusting for years even when irons are stored in a seasonal environment where they sweat with changes in temperature and humidity. Surfaces treated with linseed oil can always be easily cleaned by wire wheel buffing.

(4) Painting of irons is not recommended because it adversely affects resale potential. Paint touch-up to a handle or other originally painted surface, however, can often enhance the appearance and value of an iron.

NOTE - Surface treatment of the irons in your collection will always be a personal preference. My preference is to maintain the original surface patina except for mild cleaning and rust inhibiting. Generally, this approach will ensure that the irons will still be desirable to the next owner.

HOW TO USE THIS BOOK

This book was prepared to be an easy-to-use reference tool for collectors and antiques dealers. The index is a key to usability, with numbers referring to the pictures, not the pages. Color pictures have a C prefix next to the numbers. Each caption refers to subjects in the pic-ture as **(L)** for left, **(M)** for middle, and **(R)** for right. If more than three subjects are pictured, the reference is from the left - i.e., **(L-1)**, **(L-2)**, **(L-3),** etc. Where front and rear are used, notations such as **(FL)** front left and **(RR)** rear right are used. The book also puts emphasis on quality pictures with captioned details about each iron. The caption details are presented in the following sequence for each iron:

- **Type** - A comment on the type of iron - i.e., polisher, machine fluter, hat iron, is given.
- **Origin** - Irons made in the U.S. are not noted. The reference to European, English or French-made irons is used.
- **Identification marks** - Patent information, numbers, and symbols cast on the iron surface in any manner is in bold print in the caption.
- **Special features** - Attention is given to those construction and/or use features that make the iron special. Routine mention of the construction materials is not made.
- **Age** - I have tried to give a general dating of each iron when no identifying dates are found on the iron. I used the approach such as mid 1800, late 1800, early 1900.
- **Length** - The length of each iron is given to the nearest $^{1}/_{8}$", such as L 5 $^{1}/_{8}$". If another measurement is important, it is noted - i.e., goffering iron barrel length (B 5") or longest barrel (LB 7").
- **Rarity** - Rarity in this book refers to the availability of this iron to a collector. The rarity scale is as follows:

> R1 - This is a common iron to find; one shows up at almost every major flea market such as the New England Brimfield Market.

R2 - To find this iron you may have to hunt at several major flea markets before you find one.

R3 - This iron is considered hard-to-find and you may hunt at shows and flea markets for several years to find one.

R4 - This iron is very difficult to find and you may find one every 5 - 10 years.

R5 - This iron is very rare. It is known in major collections; you may find one in a lifetime.

- **Value** - The value index is based upon the comments contained in **Factors Affecting the Value Index** section of this book which follows. With this in mind, I have applied the following values:

V1 - $5-10	V7 - $100-150
V2 - $10-20	V8 - $150-200
V3 - $20-30	V9 - $200-300
V4 - $30-50	V10 - $300-500
V5 - $50-70	V11 - $500-750
V6 - $70-100	V12 - over $750

- **Ownership** - Irons pictured from other collections are noted (Carson) for Buck Carson. The irons in my collection are not noted. All owners are identified below:

Mary and Richard Balestri	Linda and Charles Herrick
Charlotte and Bruce Baumunk	Anne and Paul Holtzman
Robert Borsch	Estelle and Stan Hopmeyer
Ken and Valerie Brookwell	Elizabeth and John Irons
Buck Carson	Margie and Dick Kelley
Bernie Dreher	Delyte and John McClure
Fred Eubanks	LG and Darlene Sinclair
Arlene and Jerry Fingerman	Carol and Jimmy Walker
William and Mary Furnish	

FACTORS AFFECTING THE VALUE INDEX

The value of an iron is controlled by three factors: **rarity, desirability** and **condition**.

Rarity - Rarity refers to the availability of the iron to collectors. Many factors enter into why an iron may be rare. Was the iron mass produced? Was it a desirable iron to use? How many were sold? Did it survive normal use and aging conditions? The bottom line is how many survived until they were found and saved by a collector or antiques dealer. How many are available today and how frequently one shows up for sale determines the rarity.

Desirability - Hand in hand with rarity is the desirability factor. This refers to an individual's preference in wanting to collect or own a specific iron. A good example of an iron that is highly desirable is the Silver Streak Pyrex electric iron. Not rare by any means, one Silver Streak will usually show up for sale at every major Brimfield type market. However, the Silver Streak is very desirable because of its color and Art Deco look. Accordingly, this iron has a rarity of R1 but a high value rating of V12. In contrast, if I wanted to find a dated all-wrought iron, handmade by a blacksmith, I may have to look for years. I've found two in over 30 years of collecting, but such an iron is worth only a V8 value rating while it's rarity rating is R5. Desirability is very subjective and I do not give a special scale for this factor. I do, however, give collectors hints for each category, which reflects my experience and preferences. Remember, collect what **you** like.

Condition - The condition of each iron is a major factor in establishing actual value, and in particular, in deciding whether or not to purchase an iron or wait until another can be found in better condition. Most often condition is the least important factor if the iron is rare and much desired. I would always buy (price always a factor) the very rare irons in poor condition or with missing parts if I did not have them in my collection. Some irons you may never see again and parts can be hand crafted.

In this book, I consider the condition of irons pictured to have normal use and wear; or, in other words, these irons are given a value rating based on a "good to very good" condition regardless of the condition of the iron pictured. The specific iron pictured in this book may have pitting, or missing parts, but the value rating is based upon a complete iron in very good condition. Naturally, an iron in the original box and with packing documents commands a premium value above the given value rating.

SELLING IRONS TO AND BUYING FROM THE AUTHOR

I am always interested in buying the unusual and rare irons, **even those I already have in my collection**. Entire collections are also wanted. There are many known irons that are not pictured in this book and others that will be newly discovered as one-of-a-kind. As guidance, I am interested in: (1) the unusual irons that I pictured from other collections, (2) pictured irons in general with a value index above V7 ($150), and (3) any different irons similar to those pictured and having a V7 or greater value. In addition, we have a large inventory of irons for sale at our antique shop, along with our displayed collection. An **Irons For Sale List** is published annually. To discuss details, please contact me at 233 Covered Bridge Road, Northampton, PA 18067, (610) 262-9335.

C1 (L) Slug, **PAT. APD. FOR**, pat. by Daniel Barnes, New York City, Dec 11, 1877, small swan is latch, top lifts off for slug, L 7", R5, V12 (J. Irons)
(R) Slug, like (L), gold painted top, L 7 ¹/₂", R5, V12

C2 (L) Slug, ox tongue, French, wrought and pieced construction, elaborate gate *[see (R)]*, wrought companion trivet has wonderful design and paw feet, early 1800, L 9", R5, V12
(R) Slug, ox tongue, back gate for (L), applied brass swag on gate and iron arch with brass Napoleon type figure in arch, an exceptional gate design

C3 (L) Slug, European, with brass cut work and engraved overlay plate on top, decorative cast posts, about 1850, L 7", R5, V12 (Brookwell)
(R) Slug, Danish, **J. H. 1754**, engraved brass, assay stamp on gate, L 5 ¹/₄", R5, V12 (Brookwell)

C4 (L) Triple Goffer, English, wonderful highly turned standard and support rods, with barrel plugs, mid 1800, Ht 14", LB 10", R5, V12 (Brookwell)
(R) Miniature Sad Iron, European, steel with silver inlay, late 1800, L 2", R5, V12 (Brookwell)

C5 Fluting Board, Danish, **M.I.D. 1801**, very rare fluter in oak and fruitwood, from Jutland, Roll 6 ¹/₂", R5, V12 (Brookwell)

C6 (L) Single Goffer, English, iron barrel with brass inlay, brass standard and base, wonderful form, mid 1800, Ht 10 ¹/₂", B 8", R5, V12 (Hopmeyer)
(M) Single Goffer, English, iron barrel, brass parts, with heater, mid 1800, Ht 9", B 5 ¹/₂", R4, V10 (Hopmeyer)
(R) Single Goffer, English, copper barrel with wrought monkeytail spiral and elaborate tripod base, 1700's, Ht 8 ¹/₄", B4", R5, V12 (Hopmeyer)

C7 Fluting Box, English, **P.C.**, very rare set has fluting machine and 2 boards with rollers, inlaid in various woods, late 1700, Box L 8", R5, V12 (Brookwell)

C8 Slug, German, very rare, handmade with brass overlay depicting a stag, 1600's, L 5 ³/₄", R5, V12 (Brookwell)

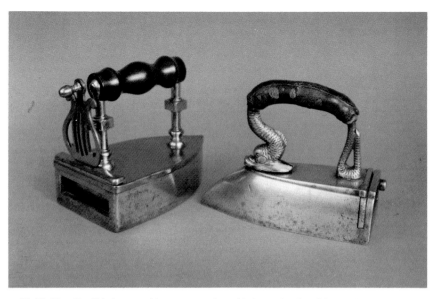

C9 (L) Slug, English, brass and iron construction with decorative lyre lift gate, late 1800, L 7 7/8", R5, V12 (Walker)
(R) Slug, German, all brass with dolphin post, leather grip, late 1800, L 8 3/8", R5, V12 (Walker)

C10 Rocking Natural Gas Heater, German, **DCGG DESSAU DRP No. 5376**, rocks back and forth to heat lower iron while upper iron is in use, late 1800, Ht 11 1/4", R5, V12 (Walker)

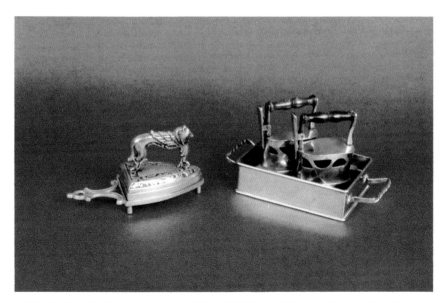

C11 (L), Slug, English, grip is feathered Lion of St. Marks, all brass with companion trivet, mid 1800, L 3 3/8", R5, V12 (Walker)
(R) Pair of Charcoal, Dutch, all brass with open work, companion trivet, late 1800, L 3 3/4", R5, V12 (Walker)

C12 (L) Triple Goffer, English, wonderful form and design, all brass, smaller barrels on horizontal arms, mid 1800, Ht 13 1/4", LB 5 7/8", R5, V12 (Walker)
(R) Mushroom Iron, English, all brass heated with slug, mid 1800, Ht 10 1/2", Dia 2 7/8", R5, V12 (Walker)

C13 Slug, European, round back, early pieced body, elaborate cutout gate with initials **W.C.** and **C.E.**, possibly a wedding gift, **1881** inlaid in brass dots on gate, L 6 ¾", R5, V12

C14 Slug, European, all brass with elaborate dolphin posts and open work lyre above gate, wonderful workmanship, mid 1800, L 7", R5, V12

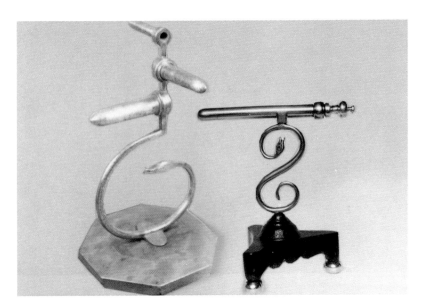

C15 (L) Triple Goffer, English, swan head decoration, on softwood base, mid 1800, Ht 19", LB 5", R5, V12 (Brookwell)
(R) Single Goffer, English, brass barrel, plug, standard, and feet, swan's head at end of "S" standard, mid 1800, Ht 8", B 7", R5, V12 (Brookwell)

C16 (L) Single Goffer, English, all brass, unique standard, mid 1800, Ht 11", B 5 ¼", R5, V11
(M) Triple Goffer, English, ornate base, all brass, mid 1800, Ht 15 ¾", LB 6", R5, V12
(R) Double Goffer, English, all brass, ball feet, mid 1800, Ht 13", LB 6 ¼", R5, V12

C17 (F) Smoothing Board, Icelandic, great geometric decoration on hard wood, 1700's, L 19", R5, V12 (Brookwell)
(M) Smoothing Board, Icelandic, **1742**, very decorative carved pine board, L 24", R5, V12 (Brookwell)
(R) Smoothing Board, Icelandic, **E.I.P.Y 1785**, dog head carved and decorated fruitwood board, L 24", R5, V12 (Brookwell)

C18 (L) Slug, English, **A. 1742**, all brass, unusual animal face at bottom of each post, floral engraving on top and sides, L 5 ⅝", R5, V12 (Hopmeyer)
(R) Slug, English, all brass, top is embossed with a vase and flowers, posts terminate with serpents, early 1800, L 6 ½", R5, V12 (Hopmeyer)

C19 Slug, Danish, bronze cast box iron with wonderful Rococo decoration depicting Mercury on the top, cast Nurnberg nymphs for uprights, about 1750, L 6 ½", R5, V12

C20 (L) Charcoal, French, Breton style, delicate cut work sides and back with **A.M.**, early 1800, L 7 ½", R5, V12 (Brookwell)
(R) Slug, Scandinavian, **H.F. SKAD 1709**, round front, cast bronze, engraved with a scorpion on top, L 5 ¼, R5, V12 (Brookwell)

11

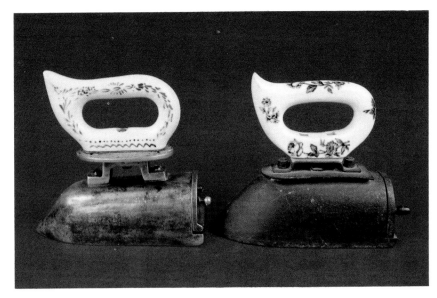

C21 **(L)** Slug, European, all brass, Delft handle, late 1800, L 7 ³/₄", R5, V12 (Carson)
(R) Slug, European, iron body, Delft handle, late 1800, L 8 ¹/₄", R5, V11

C22 **(L)** Double Goffer, English, all brass, wonderful form with paw feet, mid 1800, Ht 12", LB 7", R5, V12 (Carson)
(R) Triple Goffer, English, brass arm, cast base, wonderful layout of 3 different size barrels, one barrel plug, mid 1800, Ht 14 ¹/₂", LB 7 ¹/₂", R5, V12

C23 **(L)** Slug, Scottish, iron body with brass "S" posts, knobs, and companion brass trivet, after 1850, L 4", R5, V12
(R) Slug, Scottish, iron body with brass "S" posts, knobs, and companion brass trivet, after 1850, L 6 ¹/₈", R5, V12

C24 **(L)** Machine Fluter, **KNOX STANDARD A-1, AM FLUTING MACHINE, RUDOLPH FELDER, MACHINIST, NEW YORK**, elaborate stencil and pinstriping, picture of woman in oval, about 1875, Roll 5 ³/₄", R5, V10
(R) Machine Fluter, **HOLLY MFG CO, LOCKPORT, NY, PAT MAY 6, 1873, E.P. HOLLY**, handle disengages roll to insert heater, paint decoration, Roll 5", R5, V11

C25 (L) Drop-In-The-Back Slug, European, early pieced iron construction with cut work, companion brass trivet, early 1800, L 6 ¼", R5, V11
(R) Flat Iron, French, brass posts and companion brass cut work trivet, top surface has flowers and an urn, early 1800, L 6 ½", R5, V10

C26 (L) Slug, European, iron body with elaborate cut work in brass applied to the top surface, cutwork initials **A.I.**, hinged gate, late 1800, L 7 ⅝", R5, V12
(R) Slug, ox tongue, European, all brass with detailed dolphin post, hinged gate, late 1800, L 7 ¾", R5, V11

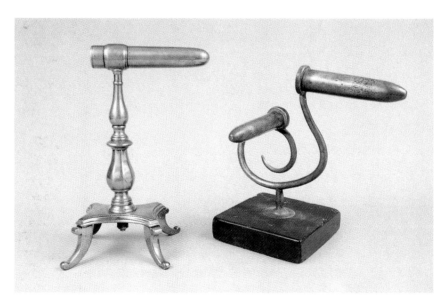

C27 (L) Single Goffer, English, all brass, unusual flared feet, mid 1800, Ht 11", B 6", R5, V12
(R) Double Goffer, English, all brass on marble base, mid 1800, Ht 10 ¼", LB 5 ½", R5, V12

C28 (L) Slug, English, all brass with engraved **(ram)** and **1884**, L 6 ⅜", R5, V11
(R) Slug, European, all brass, engraved with flowers, **1835**, hinged gate, L 5 ¼", R5, V11

C29 (L-1) Single Goffer, English, brass barrel and "S", iron base, mid 1800, Ht 7 1/4", B 6 3/4", R5, V10
(L-2) Single Goffer, English, all brass, unusual use of ring turnings with barrel plug, mid 1800, Ht 11",
B 6 1/2", R5, V11
(L-3) Single Goffer, English, brass barrel, feet are small boots, a massive iron, mid 1800, Ht 12 3/4",
B 6 1/4", R5, V12
(L-4) Single Goffer, English, iron barrel on brass stepped base with paw feet, mid 1800, Ht 6 3/4",
B 5 1/2", R5, V11

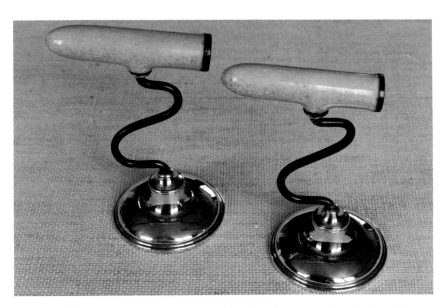

C30 Pair Single Goffers, English, rare enameled barrels with brass overlay on iron base, late 1700, Ht 7 1/2", B 4 1/4", B 5 1/4", R5, V12 (Brookwell)

C31 (L) Advertising, French, embossed and painted sign, sheet metal, about 1900, Ht 13 3/4", R4, V9
(R) Sleeve Board, cherry wood, inlaid with scissors, button hole punch, seam cutter, iron, and thimble, reverse surface is scorched, late 1800, L 14 3/4", R5, V11

C32 (L-1) Single Goffer, English, brass Queen Anne style, late 1800, Ht 5", B 2", R4, V10
(L-2) Single Goffer, English, paw feet, brass, late 1800, Ht 5 1/4", B 3 1/4", R4, V10
(L-3) Double Goffer, English, brass on wood base, late 1800, Ht 8", LB 3 1/2", R5, V12
(L-4) Single Goffer, like (L-1), Ht 5 3/4", B 2 3/8", R4, V10
(L-5) Single Goffer, English, brass base, late 1800, Ht 4 3/4", B 3 3/8", R4, V10

C33 (FL) Slug, European, all brass, mid 1800, L 3 ³/₄", R4, V10
(FM) Needle Case, European, all brass, embossed hearts and iron, late 1800, L 3 ¹/₂", R5, V11
(FR) Slug, English, all brass, mid 1800, L 2 ⁷/₈", R5, V11
(RL) Slug, European, all brass, mid 1800, L 4 ¹/₈", R4, V10
(RM) Slug, English, brass with ivory handle, late 1800, L 4 ¹/₈", R5, V11 (Carson)
(RR) Charcoal, Dutch, all brass, mid 1800, L 4 ¹/₂", R5, V11

C34 (L) Slug, English, all brass with cutout heart under handle, late 1800, L 7 ¹/₂", R5, V11
(R) Slug, European, all brass with cutout heart on lift-out gate, stylized dolphin posts, late 1800, L 7 ¹/₂", R5, V10 (J. Irons)

C35 (FL) Swan, cast iron, red with black pinstriping, late 1800, L 1 ⁷/₈", R5, V9
(FM) Swan, like **(FL)**, white with blue pinstriping, L 2 ¹/₈", R5, V9
(FR) Swan, like **(FL)**, yellow with black pinstriping, L 2 ¹/₂", R5, V9
(RL) Swan, like **(FL)**, yellow with black/red pinstriping, L 2 ³/₄", R5, V9
(RR) Swan, like **(FL)**, red with white/yellow pinstriping, L 2 ³/₄", R5, V9

C36 (L) Small Iron with Brass Fish Handle, late 1800, L 3 ¹/₂", R5, V10
(M) Pyrex, electric, **SILVER STREAK, SAUNDERS, SINCE 1858**, light blue, mid 1900, L 7 ¹/₂", R5, V12
(R) Shaving Mug, **S. S. PARSONS**, tailor shop with tools of the trade, late 1800, Ht 3 ³/₄", R5, V12

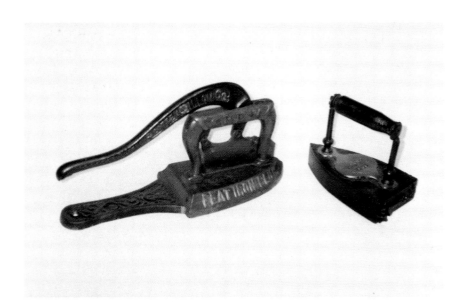

C37 (L-1) Pyrex, electric, **SILVER STREAK, SAUNDERS, SINCE 1858, MODEL 1038, 1000 WATTS, 110-120 VOLTS, AC ONLY**, a truly attractive and flashy iron, clear, mid 1900, L 7 ½", R5, V12 (Walker)
(L-2) SILVER STREAK, like **(L-1)**, red, R1, V12 (Walker)
(L-3) SILVER STREAK, like **(L-1)**, green, R5, V12 (Walker)
(L-4) SILVER STREAK, like **(L-1)**, blue, R1, V12 (Walker)

C38 (L) Tobacco Cutter, **SCOTTEN DILLON CO, CHEW FLAT IRON PLUG**, late 1800, L 16 ¼", R5, V12 (Fingerman)
(R) Slug, **W.V.W. 1800**, ornate latch characteristic of early Pennsylvania Dutch iron locks, brass plate with date, L 7 ½", R5, V12 (Fingerman)

C39 (L-1) Gasoline, **COLEMAN MODEL No. 5**, green, about 1930, L 7 ⅝", R4, V9 (Carson)
(L-2) Gasoline, **COLEMAN LAMP & STOVE CO, TORONTO, CANADA, MODEL 4A**, red, about 1930, L 8", R5, V10 (Carson)
(L-3) Gasoline, **AMERICAN No. 67, AMERICAN MACHINE CO**, tan, about 1930, L 6 ⅞", R4, V9 (Carson)
(L-4) Gasoline, **COLEMAN MODEL 609** black, about 1930, L 8 ⅛", R3, V7
(L-5) Gasoline, like **(L-3)**, **No. 66**, light green, L 6 ¾", R4, V9 (Carson)
(L-6) Gasoline, like **(L-2)**, **MODEL 4A, MADE IN USA**, blue, L 8", R1, V5

C40 Display, **HOT POINT - OF COURSE YOU WANT THE BEST, SUPER AUTOMATIC $8⁸⁰, CALROD SUPER IRON $6⁰⁰, MODEL "R" IRON $3⁹⁵, THREE POUND IRON $3⁵⁰**, display with 4 different irons, Edison Electric Appliance Co., Inc., Chicago, Ill, about 1929, L 20", R5, V12 (Balestri)

16

SMOOTHING BOARDS AND EARLY IRONING DEVICES

One of the earliest ironing devices was a smoothing stone. To the untrained eye, a rubbing or smoothing stone looks nothing like a device for pressing fabric. Used centuries ago in Scandinavia, these stones are many times referred to as "slicken stones," coming from the Scandinavian word *slekji* (to smooth or polish). These smoothing stones were made of common hard materials, such as bone, stone, glass or hard wood. To use a smoothing stone, the dampened fabric was laid out on a flat surface such as a table, and then, while holding the stone in one or two hands and pressing down hard, the stone was moved across all parts of the fabric. Berney provides documented evidence of the occurrence of rubbing stones over several centuries[1].

Another early smoothing device is the smoothing board or mangle board which also has its roots in Scandinavia and Europe. The smoothing board has two components - the flat board with handle and the roller stick which is about two to three inches in diameter. To use the smoothing board, the dampened fabric is folded in panels and wrapped (rolled) tightly around the roller. Using a flat surface like a table, the smoothing board is then pressed (at right angles) down on the rolled fabric and wood roller stick. By applying pressure in a rolling manner, the fabric is pressed and then removed from the roller. These smoothing boards and rollers were made of native hard woods. Handles of special boards are often carved with the design of a standing horse. The flat upper portion of special boards was sometimes carved and/or painted with designs of stars, flowers, hearts and symbols of fertility, happiness and prosperity. These carved and decorated boards can truly be exciting and wonderful examples of early folk art and were often made as gifts or wedding presents. Boards can also bear names, initials, sayings, dates and other notable marks which make each an individual and highly treasured antique.

Mangles and linen presses were also an early method used to press fabrics. A linen press functions much like a book press and has two flat surfaces, one of which is movable via a threaded rod so that the top surface can be pressed into the bottom surface. Fabric was placed in the press and flattened with the pressure.

A box mangle is a larger device than the linen press and may even be room size. The box mangle is normally wood and has a frame containing flat surfaces, rolling rods and a box with weights over the rollers. The box with rocks or other weights presses on the rollers and presses the dampened fabric as the frame is moved back and forth. Berney provides an accounting of use of mangles in early America.

The poking stick is another early ironing device. Made in brass, iron, or a combination of the two, the poking stick is a straight poker which is heated and then passed into the folds of fabric to produce ruffs. References to the use of poking sticks during the 16th and 17th centuries are noted by Oliver St. John[7].

Collector Hints

Smoothing boards of various types from the 1700s and 1800s can still be found today. Their uniqueness and folk art decorations make them highly desirable to collect and they can be displayed attractively. The best boards have horse handles with carving and paint decorations, but any combination of these features is good to collect. Be aware that fakes of the highly decorated horse handle boards are now being made using plastics and composition materials. These boards have a good look at first glance. Look for age and wear to identify the old from the new. Smoothing stones, mangles and linen presses are unique but may be too specialized for most collectors. Poking sticks are rare and difficult to find.

1(L-1) Smoothing Stone, European, hand blown with handle, green/black glass, about 1800, Ht 6",
Dia 4 3/4", R4, V11 (Holtzman)
(L-2) Smoothing Stone, European, blown glass, green/black, about 1800, Dia 2 7/8", R4, V9 (Holtzman)
(L-3) Smoothing Stone, like (L-2), Dia 3 1/4", R4, V9 (Holtzman)
(L-4) Smoothing Stone, like (L-2), dug from river in Amsterdam, glass opalescent from chemical action,
Dia 3", R5, V10 (Holtzman)

2 Stone Iron, Korean, granite base weighs 54 lbs, late 1700, L 21 3/4", R5, V12 (McClure)

3 Stone Iron, Korean, fabric smoothed by pounding with a pair of wood bats, granite base,
early 1900, L 21", R5, V11 (Walker)

4 Dome Iron, French, early construction, convex copper top, for pressing flat collars, heated
with hot coals or a wood fire beneath iron, 1600's, Ht 13 1/2", Dia 22", R5, V12 (Walker)

18

5 (F) Smoothing Board, European, horse handle, mid 1800, L 25", R4, V10
(R) Smoothing Board, Welsh, **J. L. ANNO, 1775**, highly chip carved, decorated surface with numerous 6 ptd stars, rope edge, oak, L 33", R5, V12

6 (F) Smoothing Board, European, horse handle and carved, mid 1800, L 23 1/4", R5, V11
(R) Smoothing Board, European, horse handle, **AKJG 1842** carved in board in relief, 6 ptd stars, circles, and interlocking stars, L 25 1/2", R5, V12

7 (F) Smoothing Board, European, horse handle, highly carved board with 6 ptd stars and other designs, red paint, early 1800, L 24", R5, V11
(R) Smoothing Board, like **(F)**, green paint, early 1800, L 25 1/4", R5, V11

8 (F) Smoothing Board, European, horse handle with traces of red/green paint, early 1800, L 25", R4, V10
(R) Smoothing Board, European, horse handle, carved designs on board, red paint, early 1800, L 25 1/4", R5, V11 (Carson)

19

9 (L) Smoothing Board, European, with roller, horse handle, early 1800, L 25", R5, V11 (McClure)
(R) Smoothing Board, Norwegian, elaborate carving with horse handle, late 1700, L 22 1/2", R5, V12 (McClure)

10 (F) Smoothing Board, European, **ANO 1773**, chip carved decoration with stars, horse handle, L 23 1/2", R5, V12 (Walker)
(R) Linen Press, Dutch, wood construction, unusual bombe-shaped base with 2 drawers, mid 1800, Ht 20 1/2", R5, V12 (Walker)

11 (F) Smoothing Board, European, turned handle, common type, late 1800, L 23 3/4", R2, V6
(R) Smoothing Board, like **(F)**, L 22", R2, V6

12 (F) Smoothing Board, European, **A. JOLSTE 1875**, painted surface, L 25", R2, V7
(R) Smoothing Board, European, painted salmon, yellow, green, late 1800, L 23", R2, V6

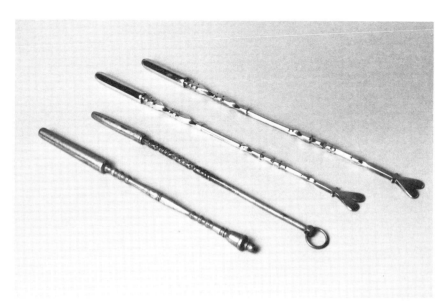

13 (F-1) Poking Stick, Scottish, steel, turned handle, urn finial, mid 1800, L 11 ¹/₂", R4, V10 (Hopmeyer)

(F-2) Poking Stick, Scottish, steel, mid 1800, L 11 ³/₄", R4, V10 (Hopmeyer)

(F-3) Pair Poking Sticks, Scottish, brass, heart finials, L 14 ³/₄", R5, V12 (Hopmeyer)

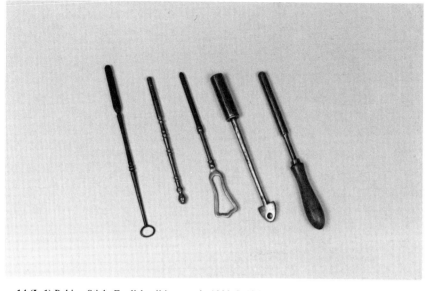

14 (L-1) Poking Stick, English, all iron, early 1800, L 12 ¹/₂", R4, V9 (Walker)
(L-2) Poking Stick, like **(L-1)**, brass finial, L 9 ¹/₂", R4, V9 (Walker)
(L-3) Poking Stick, like **(L-1)**, brass ornamental handle, L 10 ⁷/₈", R4, V10 (Walker)
(L-4) Poking Stick, French, all iron, early 1800, L 11", R4, V9 (Walker)
(L-5) Poking Stick, Dutch, iron with wood handle, late 1800, L 11 ³/₄", R4, V8 (Walker)

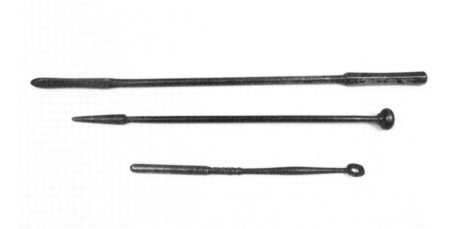

15 (F-1) Poking Stick, European, file work decoration on shaft, early 1800, L 9 ¹/₂", R4, V9

(F-2) Poking Stick, European, early 1800, L 18 ¹/₂", R4, V8

(F-3) Poking Stick, like **(F-2)**, L 14", R4, V8

16 (L) Box Mangle, Dutch, box holds rocks that put weight on the rollers, 3 wood rollers, late 1800, L 20 ¹/₂", R4, V12 (Carson)

(R) Box Mangle, Dutch, 2 wood rollers, late 1800, L 16 ¹/₂", R4, V12 (Carson)

SLUG IRONS

The name slug iron or box iron applies to those irons that are heated by inserting a hot slug of metal into the iron cavity or box. The slug heating technique kept the bottom of the iron and the ironing area free of ashes and soot which resulted in an improved ironing practice. Tongs were used to extract the slug from the hot coal or wood fire and place it into the iron cavity. Many slugs have a hole in one end so that a hook could be used to pick up the hot slug. Slug irons are more common in England and the European countries than in America.

Typical forms of European slug irons include the ox tongue iron which is shaped like a bullet and the box iron which has high straight sides. Both styles may have a vertical or hinged gate to hold the hot slug in the iron. English slug or box irons typically have a lift-up gate. Irons having an open back with a ridge higher than the base are called drop-in-the-back slug irons. Other slug irons, especially the Scottish and American forms, require that the top of the iron be removed to insert the slug.

Collector Hints

This is a very collectible type of iron, considering the construction materials (brass and iron) as well as the type of rear latch and gate or other methods to contain the slug. Some of the more desirable slug irons are engraved or have ornamental iron work. Remember, the more decorative, the more unique. European ox tongue and English box styles are readily available and prices are still reasonable.

Scottish box irons have been reproduced and the quality is good. Other brass box irons of the English type are being made. Some Belgian drop-in-the-back irons are also being reproduced. The aging techniques used frequently pit the iron body or leave it in a heavily rusted condition. Look for wear on the iron and be cautious if the iron is heavily rusted.

17 **(L)** Box, Scottish, brass posts, latch, and companion trivet, posts are "S" shaped with arrow points, an excellent example, after 1850, L 6 1/4", R5, V12
(R) Box, Scottish, brass posts, latch, and companion trivet, after 1850, L 6", R4, V10

18 **(L)** Box, Scottish, brass posts and knobs, bold handle, after 1850, L 5 3/4", R4, V10
(M) Wood Pattern, for cast slug to be used in **(L)**
(R) Box, Scottish, brass posts and knobs, "S" style posts, after 1850, L 6 3/8", R4, V11

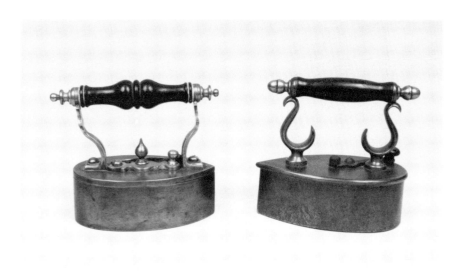

19 (L) Box, Scottish, **C. MATHER**, iron body with brass posts, latch, and knobs, after 1850, L 6", R4, V11 (J. Irons)
(R) Box, Scottish, iron body with brass "S" posts and handle knobs, after 1850, L 6 ¹/₄", R4, V10 (Carson)

20 (L) Box, round back, European, pieced construction with brass joints, lift gate with cutout top *[see* **(R)** *view]*, small acorns on rim of gate, mid 1800, L 7", R5, V12
(R) Rear view of decoration on gate

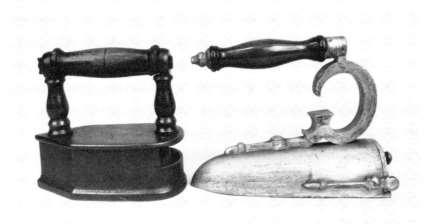

21 (L) Box, round back, European, **1855 6D JUNGE**, cut work above lift-up gate, L 8 ¹/₂", R5, V12 (Hopmeyer)
(R) Box, French, face of man on right side, sole plate extends up front, mid 1800, L 8", R4, V11 (Hopmeyer)

22 (L) Drop-In-The-Back, round back, European, early construction features, early 1800, L 6 ⁷/₈", R4, V9 (Holtzman)
(R) Ox Tongue, European, acorns at ends of hinge and handle attachments, early construction features, early 1800, L 8 ¹/₂", R4, V10 (Holtzman)

23 (L) Box, French, unusual decorative back upright, early construction, swing gate, 1700's, L 6 ³/8", R5, V11 (Walker)
(R) Box, French, early construction, swing gate, 1700's, L 7", R5, V10 (Walker)

24 (L) Box, French, pieced construction, hinged gate, 1700's, L 6 ¹/2", R4, V9 (Carson)
(M) Box, French, pieced construction, heart latch, 1700's, L 6 ¹/4", R5, V10 (Carson)
(R) Box, European, brass with engraved flowers, early 1800, L 5", R4, V9

25 Box, Danish, bronze cast box iron with Rococo decoration depicting Mercury on the top, cast Nurnberg nymphs for uprights, 1720-1760, L 6 ¹/2", R5, V12, *[see color picture* **C19***]* (Brookwell)

26 (L) Box, German, **GB HD**, pointed toe, possibly for ironing around buttons, late 1800, L 6 ¹/2", R5, V9 (McClure)
(R) Box, round back, European, with decorative cut work above gate, mid 1800, L 5 ⁵/8", R5, V12 (McClure)

27 (L) Drop-In-The-Back, European, with companion trivet, early 1800, L 6 ¼", R4, V10 (Carson)
(R) Drop-In-The-Back, European, pieced construction, early 1800, L 6 ⅛", R4, V9

28 (L) Drop-In-The-Back, European, early pieced construction, leather handle, 1700's, L 5 ½", R4, V9 (Carson)
(R) Drop-In-The-Back, European, early 1800, L 5 ¾", R4, V9 (Carson)

29 (L) Box, English, all brass body, lift-out gate with upper cutout decoration, mid 1800, L 5 ⅝", R4, V9
(M) Box, English, #3, all brass body, lift-up gate, cut work on posts, mid 1800, L 6 ¾", R4, V9
(R) Box, English, straight sides, hinged gate, mid 1800, L 5 ½", R3, V8

30 (L) Box, English, **No. 6**, brass with wigglework decoration, mid 1800, L 5 ½", R4, V9
(M) Box, like **(L)**, **No. 3**, also decorated, L 6 ¾", R4, V9
(R) Box, English, fancy posts and attachments, all brass with wigglework decoration, mid 1800, L 7 ½", R4, V10

25

31 (L) Box, English, punched **(heart) C.S. 1862**, all brass, L 7", R4, V9
(R) Box, English, all brass, decorative brass posts, late 1800, L 7 1/4", R4, V9

32 (L) Drop-In-The-Back, European, all brass with engraving, mid 1800, L 6 3/8", R4, V10
(R) Drop-In-The-Back, European, all brass with punch work designs, mid 1800, L 6 7/8", R4, V9

33 (L-1) Box, European, all brass body, hinged gate, decorative posts, late 1800, L 5", R3, V8
(L-2) Box, like **(L-1)**, L 5", R3, V8
(L-3) Box, like **(L-1)**, pieced construction, late 1800, L 5 1/4", R3, V9
(L-4) Box, like **(L-1)**, decorated sides, late 1800, L 5 7/8", R4, V9

34 (L) Box, European, **#11**, all brass body, iron handle with wrapped leather, lift-up gate, early 1800, L 8 3/4", R4, V9
(M) Box, European, **#9**, like **(L)**, L 8", R4, V9
(R) Box, European, **#8**, like **(L)**, L 7 1/2", R4, V9

35 (L) Box, English, **#10**, all brass construction, lift-up gate, mid 1800, L 7 ³/₄", R3, V8
(R) Box, English, **#8**, like **(L)**, L 7 ¹/₄", R3, V8

36 (L) Box, English, **#0**, all brass construction, lift-up gate, after 1850, L 4 ¹/₂", R2, V7
(M) Box, English, **#3**, like **(L)**, L 5 ³/₈", R2, V7
(R) Box, English, **#5**, like **(L)**, L 6", R2, V7

37 (L) Box, English, **#10**, all brass construction, lift-up gate, late 1800, L 7 ³/₄", R2, V7
(R) Box, English, **#8**, like **(L)**, L 6 ³/₄", R2, V7

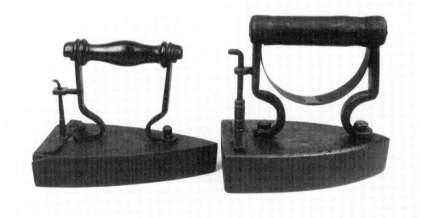

38 (L) Box, European, lift-up gate, all iron, mid 1800, L 7 ³/₄", R3, V8
(R) Box, European, all iron, heat shield, lift-up gate, late 1800, L 7 ¹/₂", R3, V8

39 (L-1) Box, English, lift-up gate, inside conduction design with a **5**, about 1900, L 6", R1, V6
(L-2) Box, English, **CRANE 4**, brass bottom, lift-up gate, late 1800, L 5 ⁷/₈", R4, V8
(L-3) Box, English, pieced construction with brass seams, mid 1800, L 5", R2, V7
(L-4) Box, like **(L-1)**, late 1800, L 4 ³/₄", R1, V6
(L-5) Box, English, like **(L-1)**, late 1800, L 4", R3, V8
(L-6) Box, English, like **(L-1)**, late 1800, L 3 ³/₈", R4, V9

40 (L) Ox Tongue, European, hinged gate, all brass, mid 1800, L 4", R4, V9 (Holtzman)
(M) Ox Tongue, European, hinged gate, fat body with companion trivet, mid 1800, L 8 ¹/₂", R4, V9 (Holtzman)
(R) Drop-In-The-Back, European, early pieced construction, brass rosette under handle post, with companion brass trivet, mid 1800, L 5 ³/₄", R4, V10 (Holtzman)

41 (L) Ox Tongue, European, wrought iron with brass French Cross on hinged gate, 1700's, L 8 ¹/₄", R5, V10
(R) Ox Tongue, European, hinged gate, late 1800, L 8 ³/₄", R3, V8

42 (L) Ox Tongue, European, wrought iron parts, some parts decorative, 1700's, L 8", R4, V9
(R) Ox Tongue, European, wrought iron parts, hinged gate, 1700's, L 7 ³/₄", R3, V8

43 (L) Ox Tongue, European, some wrought iron parts, hinged gate, 1700's, L 10", R4, V9
(R) Ox Tongue, like **(L)**, L 8 $^3/_8$", R3, V8

44 (L) Ox Tongue, European, brass body with cast iron handle, lift-out gate, mid 1800, L 7 $^1/_2$", R4, V9
(R) Ox Tongue, European, brass body with cast iron handle, lift-up gate, early 1800, L 8", R4, V9

45 (L-1) Ox Tongue, European, #2, all brass construction, lift-up gate, mid 1800, L 5 $^1/_2$", R3, V9
(L-2) Ox Tongue, European, all brass construction, hinged gate, mid 1800, L 6 $^3/_8$", R3, V9
(L-3) Ox Tongue, European, #4, like **(L-1)**, L 6 $^3/_4$", R3, V9
(L-4) Ox Tongue, European, #5, like **(L-2)**, L 7 $^1/_8$", R3, V9

46 (L) Ox Tongue, European, hinged gate, early 1900, L 8", R3, V7
(R) Ox Tongue, European, all brass body, hinged gate, late 1800, L 7 $^1/_4$", R4, V9

47 (L) Ox Tongue, European, decorated heat shield, hinged gate, late 1800, L 7 1/2", R4, V8
(R) Ox Tongue, European, all brass body, iron handle, hinged gate, mid 1800, L 7 3/8", R4, V8

48 (L) Ox Tongue, European, hinged gate, fat body, late 1800, L 7 1/8", R3, V7
(R) Ox Tongue, European, slug or gas jet heated, front vents, lift-up gate, about 1900, L 8", R2, V6

49 (L) Ox Tongue, European, hinged gate, about 1900, L 7 1/4", R2, V7
(R) Ox Tongue, German, all brass, dragon decoration, about 1900, L 6 3/4", R4, V9

50 (L) Ox Tongue, slug or gas jet heated, European, deep cast relief of a dragon spitting fire, open back, late 1800, L 7 3/4", R4, V10 (J. Irons)
(R) Ox Tongue, slug or gas jet heated, European, lift-up gate, early 1900, L 8", R2, V8

51 (L) Ox Tongue, slug or gas jet heated, German, **AVER WIEN**, front vents, lift-up gate, about 1900, L 8 ¼", R2, V7
(R) Ox Tongue, slug or gas jet heated, European, open back, front vents, about 1900, L 7 ³/₈", R2, V5

52 (L) Combination, revolving, **MAJESTIC**, pat. by Horace P. Carver, Racine, Wis, Fan 3, 1899, 4 position handle for fluting, smoothing, or polishing, L 6 ¼", R4, V10 (Fingerman)
(F) Combination, revolving, **ECONOMIST**, like **(L)**, no fluter, L 6 ¼", R4, V9 (Fingerman)
(R) Combination, revolving, **FAMILY LAUNDRY IRON**, like **(L)**, L 6 ¼", R4, V9 (Fingerman)

53 (L) Box, **BLESS-DRAKE SALAMANDER BOX IRON**, top lifts off, late 1800, L 6", R4, V9 (Holtzman)
(M) Box, **BUTTERS, PATENT FEB 13, 66**, Thomas Butters pat. of Concord, NH, top lifts off, L 5 ⁷/₈", R5, V11 (Holtzman)
(R) Box, **LAUNDRY QUEEN #2**, top lifts off, late 1800, L 6 ¼", R4, V9 (Holtzman)

54 (L) Box, **BROWN-FOSTER, MT. MORRIS NY**, 6 ptd stars on corners, lift-off top, late 1800, L 6 ¼", R4, V9
(M) Box, decorated handle grip, top lifts off, late 1800, L 5 ⁷/₈", R3, V8
(R) Box, **EMPIRE COMPANY**, flowers on corners, lift-off top, like **(L)**, late 1800, L 6", R4, V9

55 (L) Box, **L.F. DEANS**, top lifts off, front latch, late 1800, L 6 ⁵/₈", R4, V8
(R) Box, **SENSIBLE, GROTON NY**, top lifts off, front latch, late 1800, L 6 ¹/₂", R3, V8

56 (L) Box, **T.G. EISWALD, PAT NOV 15, '70**, lift-up hinged hatch for slug, L 6 ¹/₄", R5, V10
(M) Box, **S.D. HUBBARD & CO. No. 2, PITTSBURGH, PA, PAT. OCT. 1st 1867**, top lifts off, front latch, L 6", R4, V9
(R) Box, English, **KENRICK & SON LIMITED, WEST BROMWICH AKS**, hinged on side, latch on other side, late 1800, L 6 ⁷/₈", R3, V8

57 (L) Box, **PAT. APPLIED FOR**, pat. by Joel Bennitt, Defiance, Oh, top lifts off, late 1800, L 7 ¹/₂", R4, V9 (Balestri)
(M) Box, **BROOKS AND GOLDSBERRY**, top hinged at back, late 1800, L 5 ³/₄", R4, V9 (Balestri)
(R) Box, European, brass base and posts, late 1800, L 6 ³/₄", R4, V10 (Balestri)

58 (L) Combination Smoother Fluter, **N.R. STREETER**, front latch on removable handle, front hinge for slug, late 1800, L 6 ⁷/₈", R4, V9
(R) Box, **MAGIC, N.R. STREETER, PAT. SEPT 18, 1878**, rear latch on handle, with companion trivet, L 7", R4, V10

CHARCOAL IRONS

The charcoal iron is a self-heating device similar to a miniature cooking stove. Charcoal from wood or wood coals was normally used as a fuel. Heating control was provided by vents which controlled the air/oxygen supply. Less frequently, dampers for the exhaust gases were used to control the heating. Some models have numerous air vents (many always open) and other types have combinations of vents and dampers. Grates were sometimes used to allow air under the fuel, while other irons have elevated ridges cast into the bottom to improve air supply and also provide better heat conduction. European charcoal irons are characterized by numerous air vents near the bottom. Oriental charcoal irons are an open pan and are very early in origin[1]. Charcoal irons from the United States are novel and unique in design/function from the European counterparts. Vent and exhaust controls are novel in many American designs invented around 1900. Dual function charcoal irons with side and top fluters are also unique to the United States. In underdeveloped countries, charcoal irons are still widely used for pressing fabrics today. One has to wonder how charcoal irons have survived so long when considering the problems with lighting the fuel, regulating the temperature and minimizing the dirt from soot and ashes.

Collector Hints

Charcoal irons are unique and they vary in form and function. There are many, many models to collect. Prices are still reasonable for most charcoal irons and they are readily available. Some European forms are decorated with birds and people on the latches and their heat shields are often decorated. Most American models contain names and patent dates cast into the bases and, hence, aid collectors in identifying them. Reproductions of charcoal irons are found mainly in the European styles such as the brass box (with open work cutouts) and the front latch type with numerous bottom vent holes. Workmanship of these copies is poor and thin metal thickness can be a tip-off to a reproduction.

59 (L) Dragon, European, **BERLINGER**, cast dragon head, ornamental brass heat shield, hinged at back, side latch, late 1800, L 6 ⁵/₈", R4, V12
(R) Dragon, Swedish, **#2**, referred to as Husquarna, large dragon with protruding eyes, lift-off top, mid to late 1800, L 9 ¹/₂", R5, V12

60 (L) Dragon, **POMEROY PECKOVER & CO, CINN. O, PAT SEP. 7, 1854**, turned chimney is dragon head, L 11", R5, V12 (Sinclair)
(R) Box, German, **3, MUSTER SCHUTZ**, griffin latch, late 1800, L 8 ³/₄", R4, V9 (Sinclair)

61 (L) Box, European, all iron, cutouts, mid 1700, L 8", R4, V10 (Carson)
(R) Box, European, all iron, deflector heat shield for right handed use, mid 1700, L 8 ³/₄", R4, V10 (Carson)

62 (L) Box, European, brass body, iron top, fine workmanship, mid 1700, L 10", R4, V10
(R) Box, European, all iron, mid 1700, L 8 ¹/₄", R4, V10 (Carson)

63 (L) Box, Near East (old Persia), bronze, elaborate cutout work, late 1700, L 5 ³/₈", R4, V11

(R) Box, European, all iron, late 1700, L 7 ½", R4, V10

64 (L) Box, European, helmeted soldier head for front latch, hinged at back, late 1800, L 8 ¼", R3, V7

(R) Box, European, **L. LAWTON** (name punched), all brass body, riveted construction, 1700's, L 9", R4, V11

65 (L) Box, Dutch, all brass, open work at top, mid 1800, L 8 ½", R4, V10
(M) Box, like **(L)**, L 7 ⁵/₈", R4, V10
(R) Box, like **(L)**, L 7 ⁵/₈", R4, V10

66 (L) Box, German, decoration with prancing lion, hinged at back, about 1900, L 6 ½", R3, V7
(R) Box, European, hinged at back, about 1900, L 6 ½", R1, V5

67 (L) Box, European, hinged at rear, early 1800, L 8", R3, V8
(R) Box, European, hinged at rear, late 1800, L 8 3/4", R2, V7

68 (L) Box, European, **DECKEL BODEN VULKAN PATENT**, John Krist, Budapest, Austria, 1911, front latch controls top and bottom, bottom falls away to remove ashes, L 9", R5, V11 (Holtzman)
(R) Box, European, **PATENT EXPRESS**, decorated shield and top surface, top hinged at back, unusual rear damper, late 1800, L 8 3/4", R4, V9 (Holtzman)

69 (L) Fat Chimney, has extended bottom edge, late 1800, L 6 7/8", R4, V8
(M) Box, European, all brass body, referred to as the Fat Hungarian, mid 1800, L 7 5/8", R4, V9 (Carson)
(R) Box, European, odd front latch, early 1900, L 8", R3, V8

70 (L) Box, Oriental, plate with Chinese characters riveted beneath back hinge, all brass body, about 1900, L 8", R3, V7
(R) Box, European, hinged at back, early 1900, L 7 1/2", R2, V6

71 (L-1) Box, European, dolphin posts, all iron, early 1900, L 6 ⅝", R2, V7
(L-2) Box, English, **MASTER IRON**, latch missing, early 1900, L 8", R4, V8
(L-3) Box, European, black enamel, dolphin posts, late 1800, L 7 ⅝", R4, V9
(L-4) Box, European, leather handle, late 1800, L 8", R3, V7

72 (L) Tall Chimney, **W.D. CUMMINGS, E. BLESS, PATENTED 1852**, vulcan face damper, top lifts off, L 6 ⅜", R2, V6
(R) Tallest Chimney, **W.D. CUMMINGS, M. TALIAFERRO & E. BLESS, PATENTED 1852**, vulcan face damper, top lifts off, L 6 ⅝", R2, V8

73 (L) Tall Chimney, **E. BLESS, R. DRAKE, PAT'D 1852**, with vulcan face damper, pat. by Nicholas Taliaferro, Augusta, Ky & Wm. D. Cummings, Murphysville, Ky, and mfg. by Bless/Drake, Newark, NJ, L 6 ¾", R2, V7
(R) Tall Chimney, **BLESS, DRAKE, PAT'D 1852**, like **(L)**, L 5 ½", R3, V8

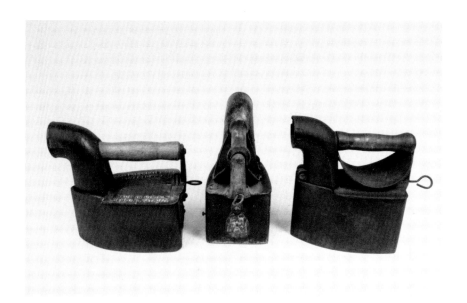

74 (L) Tall Chimney, **COLEBROOKDALE IRON CO., BOYERTOWN PA, MADE IN USA, REG. US PAT. OFF, #4**, vulcan head damper, late 1800, L 6 ¾", R3, V8
(M) Rear view of vulcan damper
(R) Tall Chimney, hinged front, vulcan face damper, late 1800, L 6 ½", R3, V8

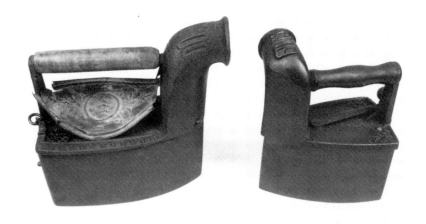

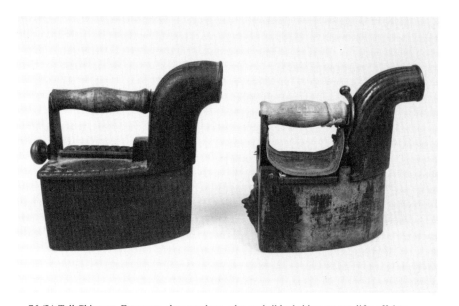

75 (L) Tall Chimney, English, **(coat of arms with lions/crown)** on decorated brass heat shield, decorated chimney, front hinge, late 1800, L 7 3/4", R3, V8
(R) Turned Chimney, European, **EDNA, PATENT NOV. 1892**, hinged at back, L 6 1/4", R2, V7

76 (L) Tall Chimney, European, decorated top edge and ribbed chimney, top lifts off, late 1800, L 6 3/8", R3, V8
(R) Tall Chimney, English, **C.V. CRANE, WOLVERHAMPTON (bird)** on decorated brass heat shield, smiley face damper, late 1800, L 6", R4, V8

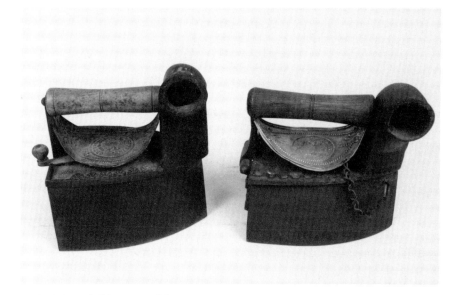

77 (L) Turned Chimney, European, **PATENT 1871, No. 1452**, lion on brass heat shield, L 7", R3, V7
(R) Turned Chimney, English, **J & J WHITEHOUSE, TIPTON #7**, phoenix bird on brass decorated heat shield, back hinge, latch under shield, late 1800, L 7", R2, V7

78 (L) Turned Chimney, English, **VICTORIA REGISTERED** with **(lions)** and **(crown seal), 7 IN**, decorated top and brass heat shield, late 1800, L 7", R3, V7
(R) Turned Chimney, English, **J & J WHITEHOUSE** Tipton, Victoria **(lions and crown seal)** on decorated brass heat shield, pin at front to release top, late 1800, L 7", R3, V7

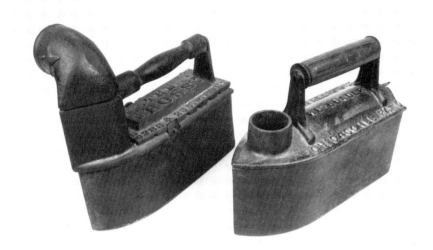

79 (L) Small Chimney, Spanish/Portuguese, hinged at back, small diameter chimney, late 1800, L 7", R3, V8
(R) Split Chimney, Spanish/Portuguese, hinged at back, chimney splits to open, late 1800, L 6 ¹/₂", R3, V8

80 (L) Turned Chimney, **THE BOSS, N.W. STOVE REP. CO, 233 & 235 W. 12 ST., CHICAGO, 22 LBS** with **(2 stars)** on turned spout, late 1800, L 11", R5, V10
(R) Stump Chimney, **STORK & KLOPP, 221 5TH AVE, CHICAGO ILL, PAT'D JULY 19, 1887**, slide damper, L 11", R5, V10 (Carson)

81 (L) Tall Chimney, adjustable side vents, chimney damper, about 1900, L 11 ¹/₂", R3, V7
(R) Turned Chimney, vulcan face damper, top lifts off, late 1800, L 11 ³/₈", R3, V8

82 (L) Box with Thermometer, Sarah Waterman, Milwaukee, Wis, pat. July 9, 1889, thermometer on brass plate, temp range 180-460° F, L 7 ³/₈", R5, V10 (Fingerman)
(M&R) Tall Chimney, one in orig wrapping, label reads **RABONE, PETERSON & CO. LTD, INCORPORATING, JOHN MORETON & CO (EXPORT SECTION ONLY), MADE IN ENGLAND**, 1931, L 6 ³/₄", R4, V9 (Fingerman)

83 (L) Double Chimney, **PAT. APPLIED FOR,** George Finn of Newark, NJ, pat. July 29, 1902, side dampers, lift-off top, L 7 1/2", R3, V8
(M) Double Chimney, **NE PLUS ULTRA, PAT'D JULY 29, 1902,** like (L), L 7 1/2", R3, V8
(R) Double Chimney, **THE ELECTRO, PAT PENDING,** six side dampers, lift-off top, early 1900, L 7 1/2", R4, V9

84 (L) Box, **PAT APPLIED FOR (10 stars),** lift-off top, side dampers, early 1900, L 7 1/4", R4, V8
(R) Box, **PATENTED AUG 18, 1914, OCT 31, 1916,** George Finn, Newark, NJ, side dampers, lift-off top, L 7 1/4", R1, V6

85 (L) Box, **PATENTED,** lift-off top, side dampers, early 1900, L 7 1/2", R1, V6
(R) Box, **THE MARVEL, PATENTED DEC 30, 1924,** side dampers, lift-off top, L 6 5/8", R1, V6

86 (L) Box, **THE PEERLESS, SELF HEATING IRON, THE AMERICAN SPECIALITY CO INC, CAMDEN NJ, PAT APP FOR,** base at back curves out, early 1900, L 7 1/4", R4, V9 (Holtzman)
(R) Box, European, **AIRA MODERNO-REGISTADO,** hinged at back, early 1900, L 7", R3, V9 (Holtzman)

87 (L) Moveable Chimney, Oriental, **KOMACHI PATENT (Oriental characters** with decoration), adjustable stack damper, after 1925, L 6 ³/₄", R2, V5
(R) Box, Peruvian, rooster for latch, 1960's, L 8", R1, V4 (J. Irons)

88 (L) Box, Argentinian, **PIETRA**, brass plated, late 1800, L 8 ¼", R3, V8 (Carson)
(R) Box, European, **PATENT NICKL METAL**, brass body, mid 1800, L 7 ¼", R3, V8

89 (L) Box, **JUNIOR CARBON IRON, 1911 MODEL, PAT APPLD FOR,** top lifts off, L 6", R4, V9 (Holtzman)
(R) Box, **THE QUEEN, CARBON SAD IRON, PAT APPD FOR, F.W. EMERSON MFG. CO, LOS ANGELES, CAL**, side vents at back, top lifts off, early 1900, L 7 ¹/₂", R4, V9 (Holtzman)

90 (L) Box, **ECLIPSE, PAT. AUG 25, 1903**, words in circle with a **(star)**, L 6 ³/₄", R2, V6
(R) Box, English, **THE BABY BOX IRON, MADE IN ENGLAND, #1, BEATRICE,** hinged back, no damper, early 1900, L 6 ³/₄", R3, V8

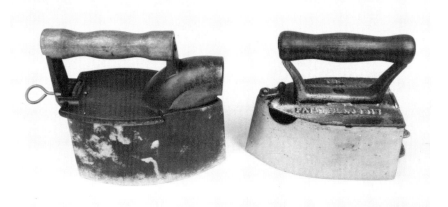

91 (L) Short Chimney, **PAT. APP. FOR**, designs on top surface, grid over chimney, slide damper, lift off top, early 1900, L 6 ⁷/₈", R5, V9
(R) Box, German, **DALLI, (GDGD in symbol)**, Gossage Co, hinged in back, early 1900, L 8", R3, V8

92 (L) Combination, short chimney, fluter plate screwed to side, top lifts off, one damper slot, early 1900, L 6 ³/₈", R3, V8
(R) Box, **THE EVER READY, PAT'D FEB 6, 1917**, an improved ACME by Margolis, top lifts off, round damper, L 6 ¹/₂", R1, V6

93 (L) Tall Chimney, **#3**, top lifts off, two hole damper, early 1900, L 6 ³/₈", R1, V5
(R) Box, **THE ACME CARBON IRON, PAT. MAR 15, 1910**, pat. by Louis Margolis, Ravenna, Ohio, round damper, L 6 ³/₈", R1, V7

94 (L) Rear Chimney, European, **FG 3**, damper in spout, hinged at back, about 1925, L 8", R2, V5
(R) Box, Mexican, **PAGOEL**, hinged at back, mid 1900, L 6 ³/₈", R2, V5

95 (L) Box, India, all brass body, numerous vent holes, front latch, back hinge, late 1800, L 8", R2, V7
(R) Box, Oriental, all brass body, side vents, front latch, back hinge, early 1900, L 7 5/8", R2, V7

96 (L) Box, India, all brass body, massive size, numerous vent holes, hinged at back, late 1800, L 10 1/2", R2, V7
(R) Box, India, like **(L)**, early 1900, L 9 1/2", R2, V7

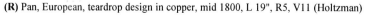

97 (L) Pan, Greek, round pan with high ridges in bottom, about 1900, L 18", R4, V8 (Holtzman)
(R) Pan, European, teardrop design in copper, mid 1800, L 19", R5, V11 (Holtzman)

98 (L-1) Pan, Oriental, bronze with designs, Oriental woman in robe carved on ivory handle, late 1800, L 12", R4, V9
(L-2) Pan, like **(L-1)**, Oriental man in robe carved on ivory handle, L 10", R4, V9
(L-3) Pan, like **(L-1)**, flowers carved on ivory handle, L 10 1/2", R4, V8
(L-4) Pan, like **(L-1)**, 19 faces carved on ivory handle, L 12", R4, V9

99 (L) Pan, Oriental, **CHINA**, bronze with horseman designs on sides, stone handle, early 1900, Dia 2 $^7/_8$, R1, V4
(M) Pan, Oriental, **CHINA**, bronze hexagonal pan with pictures of urns on sides, wood handle, early 1900, Dia 5", R3, V7
(R) Pan, Oriental, **CHINA**, bronze with dragons on sides, composition handle, early 1900, Dia 2 $^3/_8$", R1, V4

100 (L) Pan, Oriental, handle missing, bronze with open work at front edge, mid 1800, Dia 4 $^7/_8$", R3, V7
(M) Pan, Oriental, handle missing, bronze with engraved dragons, late 1800, Dia 5 $^1/_4$", R4, V8
(R) Pan, Oriental, handle missing, bronze with decoration and writing on sides, mid 1800, Dia 4", R2, V7

101 (L) Pan, Japanese, brass, about 1900, L 15", R3, V7 (Carson)
(M) Pan, Chinese, brass, decorated sides, ivory carved handle, mid 1800, L 10", R3, V8
(R) Pan, Oriental, brass, about 1900, L 11", R2, V7 (Carson)

102 (L) Pan, Oriental, brass pan with wood handle, late 1800, L 16", R2, V6
(R) Pan, Oriental, handle missing, all cast iron, made in 2 pieces, writing and decoration on sides, early 1900, Dia 7", R2, V5

GOFFERING IRONS

Goffering irons have been referred to by various names such as Italian irons, tally irons and toddy irons (which is erroneous). In this book the name goffering iron will be used. More important is the function of the iron for ruffling, frilling and pleating fabrics which was done as early as the 12th century in France[7]. In use, the poker/slug provided heat to the barrel which varied in size depending on the size of ruff desired. Ruffs were made by placing the dampened fabric on the heated barrel and then repeating the process to produce a pattern of ruffs. The use of goffering irons was mainly confined to England and the European countries. In the United States few, if any, goffering irons were manufactured. Some 20th century models like the English Kenrick or Clark goffering irons were sold via American catalogues.

Collector Hints

Goffering irons are often very decorative. Iron and brass goffering irons with Queen Anne tripod feet, bulbous turnings, and finials are like small sculptures. Wrought iron examples can be equally exciting with spiral monkeytails and exceptional workmanship. Special barrel plugs add to the overall style and form. Late forms made of iron with round bases and simple "S" wire standards signaled the end of graceful lines and craftmanship, and eventually the end of goffering iron use. The more desirable goffering irons have two or more barrels and bold, massive turnings. Round base models with "S" wire standards are still available at reasonable prices. Brass Queen Anne styles with bold turnings are now difficult to find and they are priced accordingly. No reproductions are known at this time.

103 (L) Slug for Center Well
(M) Double, English, slug in center well heated the barrels, early 1800, Ht 14 3/4", B 4 1/4", R5, V12 (Walker)
(R) Single, English, ornate open work standard and cast base, barrel plug, mid 1800, Ht 10 1/4", B 6 3/4", R5, V12 (Walker)

104 (L) Triple, English, all iron, cast paw feet, mid 1800, Ht 12", LB 8", R5, V12 (Hopmeyer)
(R) Double, English, wrought with 3 monkeytail spirals, tripod base, a wonderful example of workmanship and form, 1700's, Ht 11", LB 4 3/4", R5, V12 (Hopmeyer)

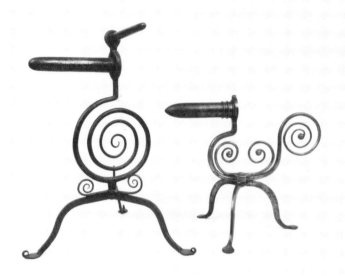

105 (L) Double, Scottish, wrought iron with tripod base and penny feet, 1700's, Ht 10", LB 5 1/2", R5, V12 (Hopmeyer)
(M) Single, English, wrought with 2 monkeytail spirals, 1700's, Ht 14 7/8", B 5", R5, V12 (Hopmeyer)
(R) Single, European, wrought with snake standard, tripod base, penny feet, mid 1800, Ht 11", B 5 1/2", R5, V12 (Hopmeyer)

106 (L) Double, European, all wrought iron, wonderful monkeytail spiral and other smaller spirals, tripod base, 1700's, Ht 15 1/2", LB 6 1/4", R5, V12
(R) Single, European, all wrought iron, 3 wonderful monkeytails with copper buttons at centers, tripod base, 1700's, Ht 10 1/2", B 5 1/2", R5, V12

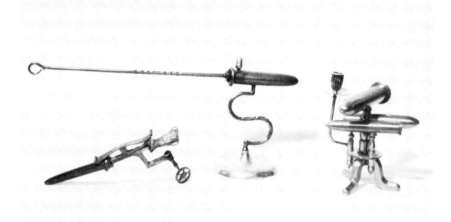

107 (L) Clamp-On, reported to be from Philadelphia, PA, 1826, barrel breaks down like a shotgun to remove heater, B 5", R5, V12 (McClure)
(M) Single, English, brass base, iron barrel, brass acorn on barrel locks heater in, mid 1800, Ht 9 3/4", B 6 1/4", R5, V12 (McClure)
(R) Triple, Scottish, has candle holder, brass standard, mid 1800, Ht 9", LB 7 1/2", R5, V12 (McClure)

108 (L) Single, European, wrought with flat iron monkeytail spirals, 1700's, Ht 8", B 4 3/8", R5, V12 (Hopmeyer)
(R) Single, European, wrought with flat monkeytail spiral, 1700's, Ht 9 1/2", B 4", R5, V12 (Hopmeyer)

109 (L) Single, European, brass barrel and standard, decorative cast base, with plug, early 1800, Ht 12", B 8 1/4", R5, V12 (Sinclair)
(R) Double, European, wrought iron with spider base, 1700's, Ht 8", LB 4", R5, V12 (Sinclair)

110 (L) Double, European, all wrought, with heater, tripod base, nice monkeytail, 1700's, Ht 10 3/4", LB 4 3/4", R5, V12
(M) Single, European, all wrought, tripod base, monkeytail, 1700's, Ht 9", B 5", R5, V11
(R) Single, like **(M)**, Ht 7 1/4", B 4", R4, V10

111 (L) Single, European, all wrought iron, small monkeytail, tripod base, early 1800, Ht 11", B 4 3/8", R4, V11
(R) Single, European, base wrought, barrel and standard turned, nice spiral end on feet, early 1800, Ht 8 3/8", B 5 1/2", R5, V12

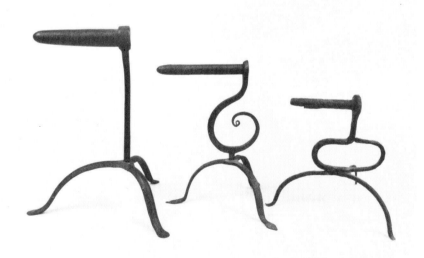

112 (L) Single, European, all wrought iron, tripod base, early 1800, Ht 9", B 4 1/2", R3, V9
(M) Single, European, all wrought iron with small monkeytail, 1700's, Ht 7 1/2", B 4 5/8", R4, V10
(R) Single, European, all wrought, tripod base, 1700's, Ht 6 1/8", B 3 1/2", R4, V10

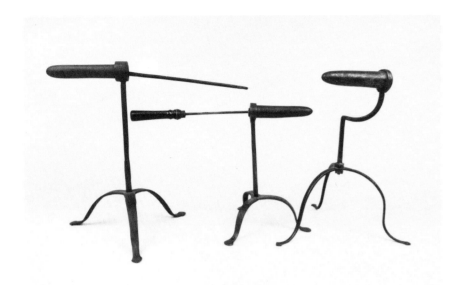

113 (L) Single, European, all wrought iron, tripod base, 1700's, Ht 12 $\frac{1}{2}$", B 5 $\frac{1}{2}$", R4, V9
(M) Single, like **(L)**, Ht 9 $\frac{1}{4}$", B 4 $\frac{5}{8}$", R4, V9
(R) Single, like **(L)**, delicate form, 1700's, Ht 12 $\frac{1}{4}$", B 5 $\frac{5}{8}$", R5, V10

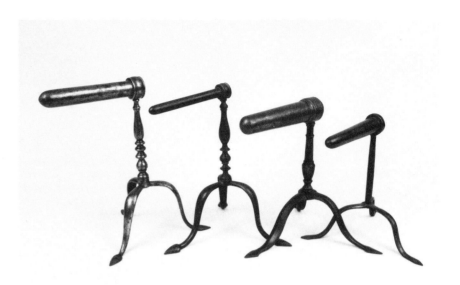

114 (L-1) Single, European, all iron, tripod base with arrow tipped feet, mid 1800, Ht 9 $\frac{1}{2}$", B 5 $\frac{1}{2}$", R4, V9
(L-2) Single, like **(L-1)**, Ht 9", B 4 $\frac{7}{8}$", R4, V9
(L-3) Single, like **(L-1)**, Ht 8 $\frac{1}{4}$", B 5 $\frac{1}{2}$", R3, V8
(L-4) Single, European, all wrought, tripod base with pointed feet, early 1800, Ht 7 $\frac{1}{2}$", B 4 $\frac{1}{2}$", R3, V8

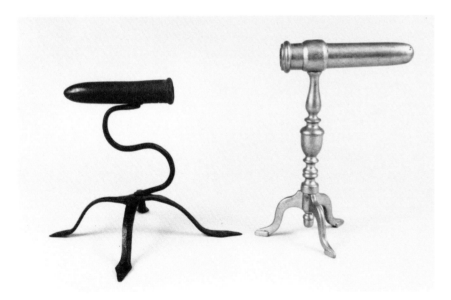

115 (L) Single, European, wrought with spider base, mid 1800, Ht 7 $\frac{1}{2}$", B 4 $\frac{3}{4}$", R4, V10
(R) Single, English, brass, Queen Anne with tripod base, mid 1800, Ht 8 $\frac{3}{4}$", B 5 $\frac{3}{4}$", R3, V9

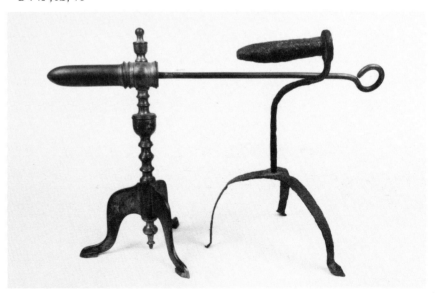

116 (L) Single, English, all iron, high Queen Anne style tripod base, Ht 12 $\frac{3}{4}$", B 5 $\frac{7}{8}$", R4, V10
(R) Single, European, wrought iron, tripod base, early 1700, Ht 12", B 4 $\frac{7}{8}$", R4, V10

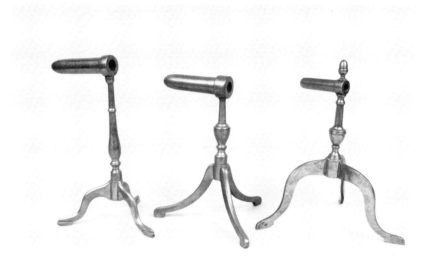

117 (L) Single, English, all brass with Queen Anne tripod base, mid 1800, Ht 10 ³/₈", B 5", R3, V9

(M) Single, English, all brass, tripod base, mid 1800, Ht 9 ¹/₄", B 4 ³/₄", R3, V9

(R) Single, like **(L)**, unusual high base, mid 1800, Ht 10 ¹/₄", B 3 ¹/₄", R4, V10

118 (L) Single, English, all brass with tripod Queen Anne base, very tall iron, mid 1800, Ht 16 ¹/₂", B 5 ⁷/₈", R5, V10

(M) Triple, European, all iron, 2 barrels bolted on standard, open work designed cast iron base, early 1800, Ht 12 ¹/₄", LB 7 ³/₄", R5, V12

(R) Single, English, all brass, unstable with small base, a missing base part?, mid 1800, Ht 10 ³/₈", B 7", R3, V8

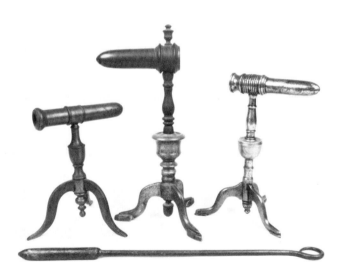

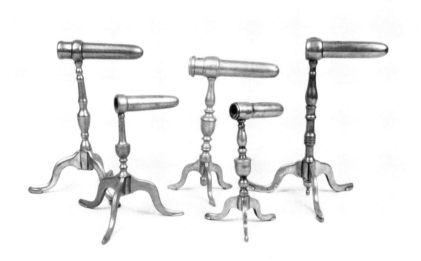

119 (L) Single, English, all brass, tripod base, late 1800, Ht 8", B 6", R3, V9

(M) Single, English, iron barrel and top half of standard, brass Queen Anne tripod base and bottom of standard, massive standard, mid 1800, Ht 12 ¹/₂", B 5 ¹/₄", R5, V11

(R) Single, English, all iron except center brass bulbous turning, Queen Anne tripod base, mid 1800, Ht 9 ¹/₂", B 5 ⁵/₈", R4, V10

120 (L-1) Single, English, all brass Queen Anne style tripod base, mid to late 1800, Ht 9 ¹/₂", B 5", R3, V9

(L-2) Single, like **(L-1)**, Ht 7", B 3 ⁵/₈", R3, V9

(L-3) Single, like **(L-1)**, Ht 8 ¹/₄", B 5 ¹/₂", R3, V9

(L-4) Single, like **(L-1)**, Ht 6 ³/₄", B 3 ¹/₄", R3, V9

(L-5) Single, like **(L-1)**, Ht 10", B 4 ⁷/₈", R3, V9

49

121 (L-1) Double, English, all brass with Queen Anne tripod base, mid 1800, Ht 12 ³/₄",
LB 4 ⁷/₈", R4, V10

(L-2) Double, English, like **(L-1)**, Ht 11 ¹/₄", LB 5 ¹/₄", R4, V10

(L-3) Double, English, like **(L-1)**, Ht 13 ¹/₄", LB 5 ¹/₄", R4, V10

122 (L) Single, English, iron barrel, brass standard and Queen Anne tripod base, mid 1800,
Ht 6 ⁷/₈", B 3 ¹/₄", R3, V9

(M) Single, English, all iron, tripod base, mid 1800, Ht 7 ³/₄", B 3 ⁵/₈", R3, V9

(R) Single, English, all brass with Queen Anne tripod base, mid 1800, Ht 6 ¹/₂", B 5 ¹/₄", R3,
V9

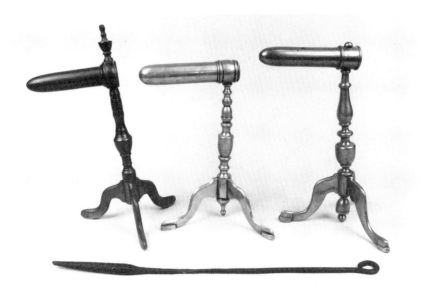

123 (L) Single, English, all brass with Queen Anne tripod base, mid 1800, Ht 11 ⁷/₈",
B 4 ⁷/₈", R3, V9

(M) Single, like **(L)**, Ht 9 ³/₄", B 5 ⁵/₈", R3, V9

(R) Single, like **(L)**, Ht 10 ¹/₂", B 5 ⁵/₈", R3, V9

124 (L) Single, English, all brass, "S" standard and round base, with heater, mid 1800,
Ht 8 ³/₄", B 6 ¹/₂", R4, V10

(M) Single, like **(L)**, Ht 8 ¹/₂", B 5 ¹/₂", R4, V10

(R) Single, English, all brass, odd standard, round base, mid 1800, Ht 7 ¹/₄", B 5 ¹/₂", R4,
V10

125 (L) Single, English, all brass with open work cast brass base, late 1800, Ht 8", B 3 ½", R4, V10 (Holtzman)
(M) Single, English, all brass, late 1800, Ht 6 ½", B 4 ½", R4, V10 (Holtzman)
(R) Double, English, all brass, late 1800, Ht 6 ½", LB 4 ½", R5, V12 (Holtzman)

126 (L) Double, European, brass barrels and standard, ornate cast iron base, mid 1800, Ht 10", LB 6 ⅞", R4, V10
(R) Double, European, iron barrels and standard, ornate cast iron base, mid 1800, Ht 10 ½", LB 5 ⅛", R4, V10

127 (L-1) Double, European, all iron, ornate cast iron base, mid 1800, Ht 18 ½", LB 7", R4, V10
(L-2) Double, European, brass barrels and upper standard, ornate cast iron base, iron lower standard, mid 1800, Ht 14", LB 6 ⅛", R4, V10
(L-3) Double, like **(L-1)**, with hole plugs, Ht 14 ¼", LB 7", R4, V11
(L-4) Double, European, all brass with ball feet, mid 1800, Ht 15", LB 5 ⅛", R5, V11

128 (L) Double, European, all iron barrels and standard, ornate cast iron base, mid 1800, Ht 11 ½", LB 5 ⅛", R4, V10
(R) Single, European, iron barrel, brass standard, ornate cast iron base, mid 1800, Ht 11 ¼", B 5 ⅜", R4, V10

51

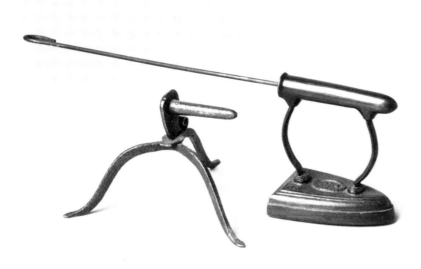

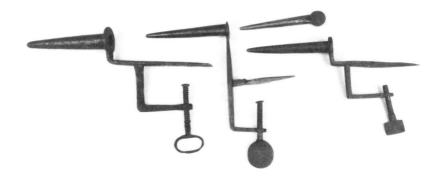

129 **(L)** Single, European, wrought, Ht 5 ¹/₂", B 3 ¹/₂", R5, V11 (Hopmeyer)
(R) Combination, English, **MFG. BULLOCK**, flat iron with goffering iron as handle, about 1900, Iron L 5", R5, V12 (Hopmeyer)

130 **(L-1)** Clamp-On, European, all wrought, heart design on thumbscrew, 1700's, B 4 ³/₄", R5, V11
(L-2) Clamp-On, European, all wrought, with plug heater, 1700's, B 4 ¹/₂", R4, V10
(L-3) Clamp-On, like **(L-2)**, 1700's, B 4 ¹/₂", R4, V10

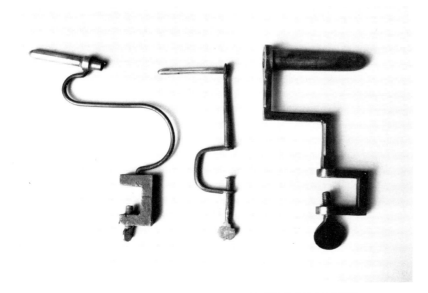

131 **(L)** Clamp-On, European, brass barrel, iron clamp, mid 1800, B 3 ¹/₂", R5, V12 (Hopmeyer)
(M) Clamp-On, European, brass barrel with wrought clamp, heart shaped screw, early 1800, B 3 ¹/₄", R5, V12 (Hopmeyer)
(R) Clamp-On, European, all iron, late 1800, B 4 ⁷/₈", R4, V11 (Hopmeyer)

132 **(L)** Single, European, iron barrel and standard, cast iron base, late 1800, Ht 8 ¹/₄", B 4 ¹/₄", R3, V8
(R) Single, European, all cast iron, early 1900, Ht 8 ¹/₄", B 5 ³/₄", R3, V7

133 (L) Single, European, all iron, ornate cast base, mid 1800, Ht 9", B 7 ¹/₄", R4, V9
(M) Single, European, all brass, very bold turnings, mid 1800, Ht 7 ¹/₂", B 7", R4, V10
(R) Single, English, all iron, cast paw feet, mid 1800, Ht 9", B 5 ³/₄", R4, V10

134 (L) Single, English, brass barrel, iron standard, cast iron dome base, mid 1800, Ht 10", B 5 ¹/₄", R4, V9
(M) Single, English, all brass, mid 1800, Ht 7 ³/₈", B 6", R3, V9
(R) Single, English, brass barrel and base, iron standard, barrel plug, mid 1800, Ht 8 ¹/₄", B 5 ¹/₄", R4, V10

135 (L) Single, English, all brass, late 1800, Ht 10", B 5 ³/₄", R3, V9
(M) Single, English, all brass, late 1800, Ht 7 ¹/₂", B 6 ³/₄", R3, V9
(R) Single, English, all brass, late 1800, Ht 6 ³/₄", B 4 ¹/₂", R3, V9

136 (L) Single, English, brass barrel, iron standard and base, late 1800, Ht 10 ¹/₂", B 6 ¹/₂", R3, V9
(R) Single, European, wrought barrel and standard, cast iron base, mid 1800, Ht 8 ¹/₂", B 5 ³/₄", R3, V8

137 **(L)** Single, English, all brass, mid 1800, Ht 6 ¼", B 5 ⅝", R3, V8
(M) Single, English, brass barrel with iron collar, base top in brass, mid 1800, Ht 5 ¼",
B 4 ⅞", R4, V9
(R) Single, European, brass barrel, ornate cast iron base, late 1800, Ht 5 ¼", B 4 ⅞", R3, V8

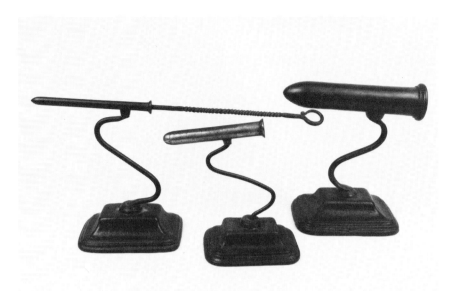
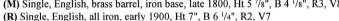

138 **(L)** Single, English, **A. KENRICK & SONS**, all iron, early 1900, Ht 6 ¼", B 5 ⅛", R3,
V7
(M) Single, English, brass barrel, iron base, late 1800, Ht 5 ⅞", B 4 ⅛", R3, V8
(R) Single, English, all iron, early 1900, Ht 7", B 6 ¼", R2, V7

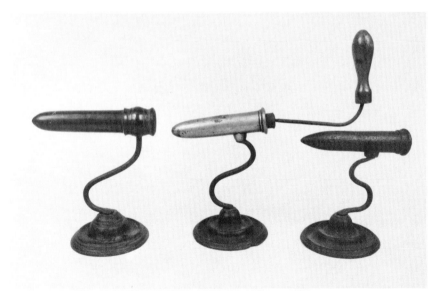

139 **(L)** Single, European, all iron, late 1800, Ht 7 ¾", B 6 ⅜", R3, V8
(M) Single, European, brass barrel with heater, late 1800, Ht 7 ⅜", B 5 ¼", R3, V8
(R) Single, European, all iron, late 1800, Ht 6 ¼", B 6", R3, V7

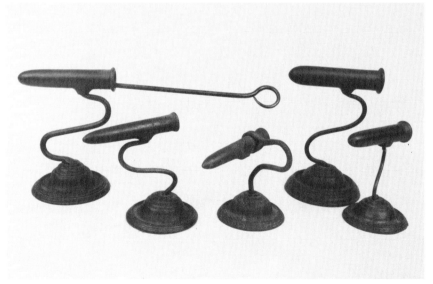

140 **(L-1)** Single, English, **W. BULLOCK & CO, #10**, "S" style standard and round base,
early 1900, Ht 6 ¼", B 4 ⅞", R1, V6
(L-2) Single, English, early 1900, Ht 5", B 4 ½", R1, V6
(L-3) Single, like **(L-2)**, make-do standard, Ht 4 ¼", B 4 ¼", R3, V6
(L-4) Single, like **(L-2)**, **CLARK**, Ht 7", B 4 ¾", R1, V6
(L-5) Single, like **(L-2)**, Ht 5", B 3 ⅝", R1, V6

FLUTERS

The invention of numerous fluting devices during the period 1860 to 1890 revolutionized previous methods for crimping, ruffling and pleating fabrics. These new fluting devices produced ruffles by pressing dampened fabric between two intermeshing, heated ribbed (fluted) surfaces. Inventors of this period produced unusual and imaginative designs - i.e., rockers, rollers, machine hand crank units, revolving combinations of fluters and flat irons, charcoal irons with fluters, fluters and slug irons, as well as models that convert from a flat iron to a fluter. The fluter period was one of invention and novelty. One fluter is convex/concave and very awkward (Dion); another has the profile of a goat (Myers); another converted a flat iron to a fluter by interchanging parts in the handle (Magic). One of the most well known machine fluters was patented by a woman, Susan R. Knox. Decoration also played a part in the fluter period. Stenciling, painting and the use of decals added to the charm of an ironing device that was mainly cast iron. Fluters are found mainly in the United States and England; but after considering all the types and patents, one has to realize that the Fluting Period belongs to the United States. The English fluters are very distinctive from those made in America. They are characterized by fine flutes while the American fluter ribs are two to three times the size of their English counterparts.

Collector Hints

If I had to confine my collecting to one type of iron, I am sure it would be fluters. A wide variety of fluters exists today and even those that are not rare have unique parts and nicely painted and stenciled surfaces. There are no reproductions in the large models (only in the very small size rockers). Focus on stenciled and decorated machine fluters in excellent condition and unusual styles. Combination fluters are very desirable and much sought after. New fluter variations that have never been seen before continue to be found - to the amazement of all collectors.

141 **(L)** Rocker, **PAT AUG 21 1868, OCT 18 1870**, Charles Dion, NY, slugs in top/bottom, brass fluter plates, L 4 ¹/₂", R5, V12 (Carson)
(R) Combination, twist handle machine, **FASHION**, F. Myers, goat profile on front, hinged at front, pat. Feb 18 '72, L 6 ⁵/₈", R5, V12

142 **(L)** Combination, revolving, **PAT 1876**, hinged door on fluter side for slug, L 5 ¹/₂", R5, V11
(R) Combination, revolving, alcohol, **PAT OCT 3rd 1882**, 4 usable surfaces, L 6 ¹/₄", R5, V11

143 (L) Combination, revolving, John Hewitt style handle, 2 sets of rollers with 6 grooves, about 1870, L 6 $\frac{1}{4}$", R5, V10
(M) Combination, revolving, **HEWITT, PAT MAR 4 1873**, removable fluter plate fastened by thumbscrew, L 6 $\frac{1}{4}$", R3, V9
(R) Combination, revolving, **MANN'S PAT**, flutes cast into body, about 1870, L 6", R4, V9

144 (L) Combination, **PATENTED**, fluter clamps on sad iron, wooden tin covered fluter base, late 1800, Plate 2 $\frac{5}{8}$ x 3 $\frac{1}{2}$", R5, V10 (Balestri)
(R) Roller, **OGDEN'S FLUTER, PAT. APPL'D FOR**, brass roller holds slug, brass covered board, base L 11 $\frac{3}{4}$", R5, V10 (Balestri)

145 (L) Combination, **PATENTED JULY 24, '74**, fluter clamps on sad iron, metal fluter base, L 8 $\frac{1}{2}$", R5, V10 (Sinclair)
(R) Combination, **CANTON MFG CO, CANTON OHIO, APR 20 1869**, fluter clamps on sad iron, wood fluter base, L 8 $\frac{3}{4}$", R5, V10 (Sinclair)

146 (L) Combination, slug, **MAGIC No. 1**, by N. R. Streeter, pat. Sept 19, 1876, with accessory 2 pc fluter, L 7 $\frac{1}{2}$", R4, V10 (Carson)
(R) Combination, slug, **MRS STREETER'S MAGIC FLUTER & POLISHER, PAT SEPT 19, 1876**, top fluter clamps on handle for fluting, handle clamps on base for ironing, L 7 $\frac{1}{2}$", R4, V10

147 (L) Combination, **PAT'D DEC 12, 1871**, pat. by Charles W. Monroe, Chicago, Ill, brass top and base plate, L 5 ⁵/₈", R4, V10
(R) Combination, **F. MYERS, PAT MARCH 7, 1871 #8**, brass top and base plates, L 5 ⁵/₈", R4, V10

148 (L) Combination, **LITTLE GIANT, PAT DEC 10, 73**, with board, 6 flutes, L 5 ³/₄", R4, V10
(R) Combination, **PATENTED DEC 73**, 7 flutes, L 6", R4, V10

149 (L) Combination, **PAT'D AUG 2, 70**, by Myron H. Knapp, Bay City, Mich, front latch and hinge, L 6 ⁵/₈", R2, V7
(R) Combination, like (L) but smaller, L 5 ⁷/₈", R2, V7

150 (L) Combination, **FEB 28, 1874**, wire clip closure, L 7", R2, V6
(R) Combination, revolving, **LADIES FRIEND, MF'D BY H.P. CARVER, RACINE, WIS**, latched door for slug, pat. Jan 3, 1899, L 7 ¹/₄", R4, V8

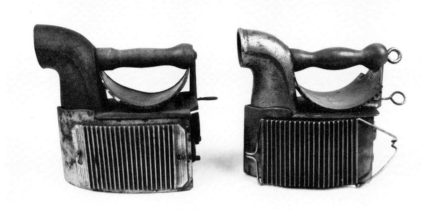

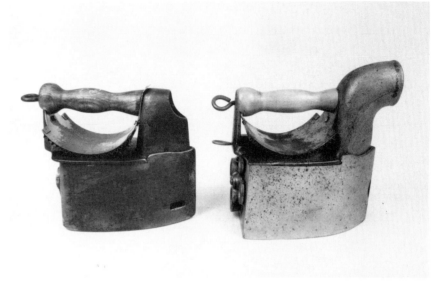

151 (L) Combination, charcoal, gold stenciled on heat shield **CLASSEN BROS & CO, ITHACA NY**, late 1800, L 7", R5, V10
(R) Combination, charcoal, **PAT AUG 18 '85** on brass heat shield which is fluter rocker, fluter plate clips on the side, L 6 ½", R4, V9

152 (L) Combination, charcoal, **PAT'D AUG 23, 1904 PAT. PEND**, chopped down chimney, fluter rocker in handle, vent in front, L 6 ¼", R3, V8
(R) Combination, charcoal, **M.S. PEASE, CINCINNATI O, PATENTED AUG 14, 1888**, fluter rocker in handle, top lifts off, L 6 ¾", R3, V9

153 (L) Combination, charcoal, **ECLIPSE, PAT AUG 25 1903**, side fluter piece and separate rocker, L 6 ½", R2, V8
(M) Combination, charcoal, **THE ACME CARBON IRON, PAT MARCH 15 1910**, Acme Self-Heating Iron Co, Ravenna, Ohio, rocker separate, L 7", R2, V8
(R) Combination, charcoal, **ECONOMY, PATENTED JULY 17 1906**, rocker separate, L 7", R3, V8

154 (L) Machine, fluter rolls are side by side, decal, late 1800, Roll 6", R5, V12 (Sinclair)
(R) Machine, single pedestal containing tension spring, late 1800, Roll 4 ½", R5, V12 (Baumunk)

155 (L) Electric Machine, **C. VIGNERON (cross** in oval) **LITTLE FERRY, NJ**, about 1900, Roll 6", R5, V11 (McClure)
(M) Natural Gas Machine, Belgium, **J. LINCENS - FIL'S CONSTRUCTEURS TOUR'ANI BELGIQUE**, gas pipe inlet hidden, late 1800, Roll 10 ½", R5, V12 (McClure)
(R) Machine, **PATENT APPLIED FOR**, triangular base, about 1880, Roll 4 ½", R5, V11 (McClure)

156 (L) Machine, stenciled **EUREKA, PATENTED FEB 7th 1871, JULY 25th 1871**, pinstriping and oval painted scene under rolls, Roll 4 ¾", R3, V9
(R) Machine, **MANVILLE, PATENT FEB 23 1869**, pinstriped yellow, green, white on black, red painted model also made in Waterbury, Ct, Roll 5", R4, V11

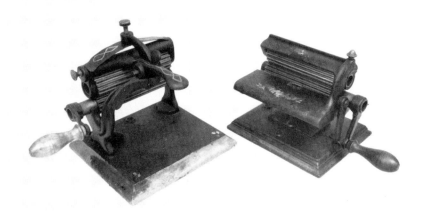

157 (L) Machine, **PERIN & GAFF MF'G CO, CIN O, MRS SUSAN R KNOX, PATENTED NOV 20 66, O**, yellow pinstriping and decals, Roll 5 ¾", R3, V9
(R) Machine, **ROYAL, PERIN & GAFF MFGS CO, CIN O, PAT MARCH 14, 1876**, red/yellow pinstriping and decals of flowers, Roll 5 ¾", R3, V8

158 (L) Machine, **CROWN, PAT NOV 2 1875, JULY 3 1877, REISSUED MARCH·23 1880, AM MACH CO, PHILA PA**, crown decal, yellow/red pinstriping on black, Roll 5 ⅞", R2, V8
(M) Machine, **CROWN, PAT NOV 2 1875, AM MACH CO, PHILA PA**, yellow/red pinstriping on black, crown decal, Roll 7 ½", R2, V8
(R) Machine, like **(M)**, Roll 5 ¾", R2, V8

59

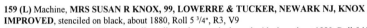

159 (L) Machine, **MRS SUSAN R KNOX, 99, LOWERRE & TUCKER, NEWARK NJ, KNOX IMPROVED**, stenciled on black, about 1880, Roll 5 ³/₄", R3, V9
(M) Clamp-On, **PRINCESS**, lower roll smaller and cannot be heated with slug, about 1880, Roll 5 ¹/₄", R5, V10
(R) Electric Machine, **PLEATING MACHINE, CIRCLE CORP, NY, PATENTED NICHOLSON FIRE CO USA**, belt or crank driven, about 1900, Roll 7 ³/₄", R5, V11 (Borsch)

160 (L) Machine, **THE ORIGINAL KNOX, PAT. JULY 3, 1877, REISSUE APRIL 26 1870, NORTH BROS MFG CO, PHILA PA**, Roll 5 ⁷/₈", R4, V9
(R) Machine, **MFG BY M. GREENWOOD & CO, CIN O, UNIVERSAL #2, PAT JULY 17 66, NOV 10 68, MAR 1 70**, caps on holes, decals on black, Roll 6 ¹/₄", R3, V9

161 (L) Machine, **THE ORIGINAL KNOX, PAT JULY 5 1877, REISSUE APRIL 26 1870, AMERICAN MACHINE CO, PHILADELPHIA PA**, red/yellow pinstriping on black, paper picture of S. Knox in oval, Roll 5 ⁷/₈", R4, V10 (Carson)
(R) Machine, **THE KNOX IMPERIAL, PAT MARCH 20, 1877, KNOX MFG CO, ASTOR PLACE NY**, with S. Knox picture, yellow pinstriping on black, Roll 6", R4, V9

162 (L) Machine, **H SAUERBIER & SON MANUFTRS, NEWARK NJ, MRS SUSAN R KNOX, PATENTED NOV 20 1866**, yellow pinstriping on black/blue, Roll 4", R3, V8
(R) Machine, stenciled **CROWN JEWEL, LOWERRE & TUCKER, NEWARK NJ, NOV 23 1869**, yellow pinstriping on black, Roll 5 ¹/₂", R3, V9

163 (L) Machine, stenciled **EAGLE**, flower decal and **PAT NOV 2 1875**, Am. Machine Co/ Albrecht's Pat., pinstriped gold on black, Roll 3 $^1/_4$", R4, V10
(R) Machine, **EAGLE, PAT NOV 2 1875, AM MACH CO, PHILA PA**, pinstriped with flower decal on black, Roll 5 $^1/_8$", R3, V8

164 (L) Machine, **AMERICAN, PAT AUG 19 1879, AMERICAN MACHINE CO, PHILADELPHIA PA**, yellow/red pinstriping on black with decals, Roll 5 $^3/_4$", R3, V8
(R) Machine, yellow/red pinstriping on black and decal of girl's face in circle, about 1875, Roll 5", R4, V9

165 (L) Machine, painted **PAT MAY ___ 187_**, yellow/red pinstriping on black, painted flowers, Roll 6", R3, V9
(R) Machine, painted ____**EIFER**, gold pinstriping on black, about 1875, Roll 5 $^5/_8$", R4, V9

166 (L) Machine, yellow pinstriping on black, decal of girl's face in circle, about 1875, Roll 5 $^5/_8$", R4, V9
(R) Machine, black painted base, about 1875, Roll 4 $^3/_4$", R3, V9

167 (L) Machine, lever at front for pressure release, about 1875, Roll 4", R4, V10 (Holtzman)
(R) Machine, **CHAMPION, KELLER & OLMESDAHL, PAT JUNE 5 1877**, stenciled and pinstriped on black, Roll 5 ³/₄", R4, V10 (Holtzman)

168 (L) Machine, English, **THE SINGER MANUFACTURING CO, GREAT BRITAIN**, plaiting and kilting, gas heated, counterweight for pressure, Roll 11", R5, V12 (Balestri)
(R) Machine, **CORRISTER'S NEW IMPROVED EXCELSIOR FLUTING MACHINE, PAT'D DEC 8 1868**, by W.D. Corrister, New York, NY, crank used for pressure, Roll 6", R4, V10 (Balestri)

169 (L) Machine, electric, **CROWN, NORTH BROS MFG CO, PHILA PA OSA, MADE IN USA**, belt driven, painted green, late 1800, Roll 7 ¹/₂", R5, V12 (Holtzman)
(R) Machine, **BANNER, MAXANT, B & S CO, CHICAGO**, could be belt driven or cranked by hand, late 1800, Roll 7 ⁵/₈", R5, V12 (Holtzman)

170 (L) Machine, **H SAUERBIER & SONS MANUFACTURERS, NEWARK NJ, MRS SUSAN R KNOX, PATENTED NOV 20 1866**, yellow pinstriping on blue/black, Roll 6", R4, V8
(R) Machine, same as **(L)**, Roll 8", R4, V8

171 (L) Machine, **STAR, PAT OCT 19 1875 (star) AMERICAN MACHINE CO, PHILADELPHIA PA,** yellow/red pinstriping on black, Roll 5 ¾", R2, V8
(R) Machine, **PENN, PAT NOV 2 1875, JULY 3 1877, REISSUED MARCH 23 1889, AM MACH CO, PHILA PA,** Roll 5 ¾", R2, V7

172 (L) Machine, pat. by Henrietta H. Cole, June 12, 1866, New York City, counterweight for pressure, painted red, Roll 5", R4, V11 (Herrick)
(R) Machine, **DIAMOND, W. CREAMER AND SON, NEW YORK,** painted red, about 1875, Roll 5", R4, V10 (Herrick)

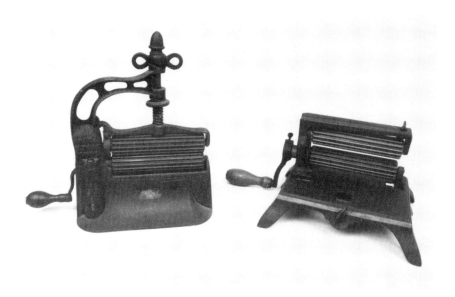

173 (L) Machine, **DUDLEY FLUTER, PATD NOV 14 1876,** red pinstriping on black, flower decals, Roll 5 ¾", R4, V10
(R) Machine, yellow pinstriping on black, about 1875, Roll 5 ¾", R3, V9

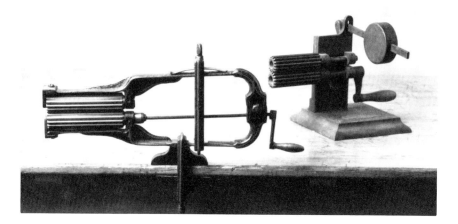

174 (L) Machine, **NIAGARA, PAT 1872,** black with red stenciling, clamps on table edge, Roll 6", R5, V12 (Hopmeyer)
(R) Machine, **BENNETT JOHNSON & CO, NEW YORK,** counterweight for pressure, red paint with gold stenciling, about 1870, Roll 4 ½", R4, V11 (Hopmeyer)

175 (L) Machine, painted red with floral pattern, large flutes, about 1875, Base 7 ½", R4, V10 (Hopmeyer)
(R) Machine, English, handmade iron frame on wood base, about 1800, Roll 4 ½", R5, V12 (Hopmeyer)

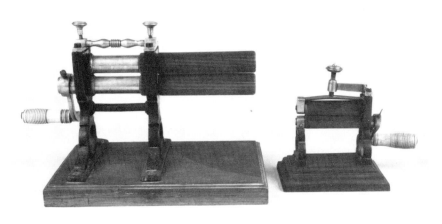

176 (L) Machine, English, fine flutes, iron frame, brass parts, ivory handle, late 1800, Roll 5 ⅝", R5, V11
(R) Machine, English, iron frame and base, brass parts, ivory handle, late 1800, Roll 3 ¼", R5, V11

177 (L) Machine, English, fine flutes, green/black base, late 1800, Roll 2 ⅞", R3, V9
(R) Machine, English, fine flutes, green base, late 1800, Roll 4 ½", R3, V9

178 (L) Machine, English, fine flutes, green painted base, late 1800, Roll 5", R4, V9
(R) Machine, English, fine flutes, black painted base, late 1800, Roll 4 ½", R4, V9

179 (L) Machine, **PAT JY 66, NOV 66**, C.S. Osborne & Co. Newark, NJ, Roll 4 ³/8", R4, V9
(R) Machine, English, brass oval tag reads **GW INGRAM, BIRMINGHAM**, large flutes, black painted frame, on wood base, Roll 4", R4, V11

180 (L) Machine, English, brass plate on base stamped **G.W. INGRAM, BIRMINGHAM** with symbols of **(lions/crown)**, green base, after 1850, Roll 4 ³/8", R4, V10
(R) Machine, English, green base, after 1850, Roll 3 ³/4", R4, V10

181 (L) Clamp-On, painted **H.B. ADAMS, PATENT PENDING**, yellow pinstriping on green, about 1875, Roll 3 ¹/2", R4, V9
(R) Clamp-On, **COMPANION**, black paint, about 1875, Roll 5", R4, V9

182 (L) Roller, **INDICATOR, PAT JUNE 4 1878, ILLION NY**, temperature pointer at end of fluter plate, L 5 ¹/2", R5, V10 (Balestri)
(R) Roller, **MADE BY HENRY A DOTY, JANESVILLE WIS, PAT'D JUNE 18 1872**, roller and base brass covered, L 6", R5, V10 (Balestri)

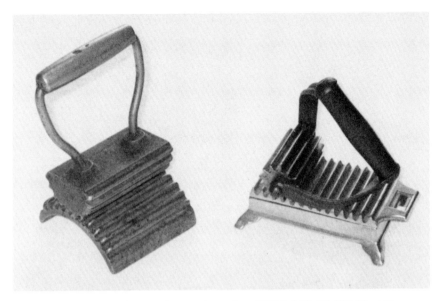

183 (L) Rocker, unusual concave/convex shape, about 1875, L 5 ¹/₂", R5, V10 (Herrick)
(R) Roller, **PAT APP'D FOR**, about 1875, L 4", R5, V10 (Herrick)

184 (L) Roller, made in a decorative style, roller holds a slug, about 1875, L 8", R4, V9
(R) Roller, crosswise roller, Norton's Improved Fluter stand, brass base plate, roller is white metal, about 1875, L 6 ¹/₄", R4, V9

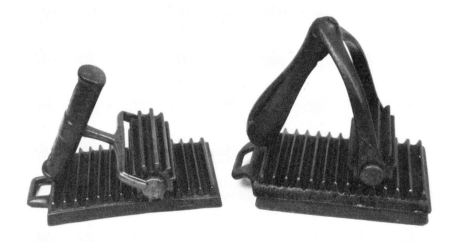

185 (L) Roller, **CLARKS, PTD '79** in script on handle, black painted surfaces, L 6 ¹/₄", R3, V8
(R) Roller, **CLARKS** on both sides of roller, black painted surfaces, about 1875, L 6 ¹/₄", R3, V8

186 (L) Roller, **PAT 1880, C.W. WHITFIELD, SYRACUSE NY, PAT APP'D FOR**, L 5 ¹/₂", R3, V7
(R) Roller, **SUNDRY MFG CO, PAT APD FOR, BUFFALO NY**, about 1875, L 5 ¹/₂", R3, V8

187 (L) Roller, **AMERICAN MACHINE CO, PHILADELPHIA PA**, hinged base plate, yellow pinstriping on black, early 1900, L 7", R1, V5
(R) Roller, same as **(L)**, roller different, L 7", R1, V5

188 (L) Roller, **N.R. STREETER'S MAGIC FLUTER & POLISHER, PAT SEP 18, 1878**, black painted surfaces, 2 pc base, L 6 ³/4", R3, V8
(M) Roller, about 1875, L 5 ³/4", R2, V7
(R) Roller, **NORTH BROS MFG CO, PHILADA PA USA**, yellow pinstriping on black, about 1875, L 6 ¹/2", R3, V7

189 (L) Roller, **PAT 1880** on handle, like **(R)**, black painted surfaces, lip on base plate and two hooks on rear, L 7 ³/4", R3, V8
(R) Roller, **SHEPARD HARDWARE CO, PAT'D NOV 12, DEC 17 1879 AND JAN 18 1880, BUFFALO NY**, hinged on base, L 7 ³/4", R3, V8

190 (L) Rocker, **GENEVA HAND FLUTER, IMPROVED, GENEVA ILL, PAT'D AUGUST 21 1866**, brass top and base plates, L 5 ³/4", R4, V10
(R) Rocker, **HOWELL'S WAVE FLUTER, GENEVA ILL, PAT'D AUG 21 1866, HEAT THIS**, brass top and base plates, flutes are in wave design, L 5 ³/4", R5, V11

191 **(L)** Rocker, **PAT AUG 21 1866**, brass base plate, L 5 ⁵/₈", R4, V8
(R) Rocker, long rocker base, all cast iron, about 1875, L 9", R5, V10

192 **(L)** Rocker, **PAT APP'D FOR**, brass top and base plates, about 1875, L 5 ³/₈", R4, V9
(R) Rocker, small fluter with base plate, holder missing, about 1875, L 4 ¹/₄", R4, V9

193 **(L)** Rocker, **THE BOSS, PAT 1882,** handle modified, L 6", R4, V9 (Holtzman)
(R) Rocker, **J. ONTON, BUFFALO NY, SB**, about 1875, L 4", R4, V9 (Holtzman)

194 **(L)** Rocker, **GENEVA HAND FLUTER, GENEVA ILL, HEAT THIS, PAT'D 1866,**
lead-like material for both parts of fluter, L 5 ³/₄", R1, V4
(R) Rocker, **THE GLOBE**, Robert Young, Hartford, Conn, patent May 29, 1883, L 5 ¹/₂",
R3, V7

195 (L) Rocker, **THE BEST, C.W. WHITFIELD, SYRACUSE NY, PAT APP'D FOR,** about 1875, L 5 $^7/_8$", R2, V6 (Carson)
(M) Rocker, **THE BEST, H. FOOTE MFG, SYRACUSE NY,** about 1875, L 5 $^1/_2$", R2, V6 (Carson)
(R) Rocker, **THE BEST,** like **(L),** tab on rocker reversed, about 1875, L 5 $^1/_2$", R3, V7 (Carson)

196 (L) Rocker, **THE LADY FRIEND, 1875,** L 6", R3, V8 (Carson)
(M) Rocker, **THE STAR,** about 1875, L 5 $^1/_2$" R3, V8
(R) Rocker, **THE (star),** about 1875, L 5 $^1/_2$", R3, B8 (Carson)

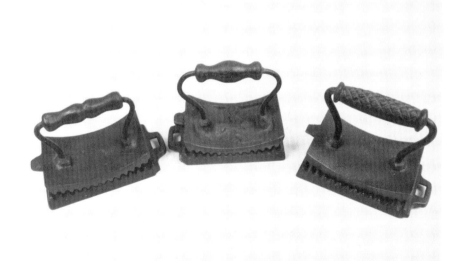

197 (L) Rocker, **THE ERIE FLUTER,** by Griswold Mfg Co, Erie, PA, clip-on handle, about 1875, L 5 $^1/_2$", R3, V7
(R) Rocker, **THE ERIE FLUTER (leaves),** late 1875, L 5 $^3/_4$", R3, V7 (Carson)

198 (L) Rocker, **MAGIC, PAT APP FOR, C.W. WHITFIELD, WATKINS NY,** about 1875, L 6", R3, V7
(M) Rocker, about 1875, L 5 $^7/_8$", R3, V7
(R) Rocker, like **(L),** different handle, L 6", R3, V7

199 (L) Roller, Dutch, wooden roller and board, mid 1800, Roller L 10 ³/₄", R4, V11 (Hopmeyer)
(R) Roller, Dutch, wooden roller and board, mid 1800, Roller L 2", R5, V12 (Hopmeyer)

200 (L) Stack, English, wood with inlaid diamonds, drawer for quills, early 1800, Ht 18 ³/₄", R5, V12 (Walker)
(R) Stack, wood with mortise/tenon construction, mid 1800, Ht 27", R5, V12 (Walker)

201 (FL) Roller, Dutch, **J. SPICER**, boxwood board/roller, mid 1800, L 6 ⁵/₈", R3, V9
(FM) Fluting Press, **W.F. GEORGE, PAT JAN 29 1861, REISSUED SEPT 15 1869**, all wood, L 5 ³/₄", R4, V9
(FR) Fluting Press, no top, mid 1800, L 10 ¹/₄", R4, V7
(R) Stack Pleater, all wood with round plaits, late 1800, Ht 11", R4, V10

202 (L) Pleater, **YOUNG'S IMPROVED PLAITER, #2, PAT MARCH 20 1877 AND SEPT 10 1879**, wood frame with hinged/clip plaits of tin, L 13 ³/₄", R2, V4
(M) Pleater, like **(L)** but larger, L 15 ¹/₂", R2, V4
(R) Pleater, **THE RIVAL PLAITER**, wood frame with loose tin plaits, paper instructions back, about 1900, R2, V4

SPECIAL PURPOSE IRONS

When considering the multitude of articles and types of fabrics that require smoothing or ironing, it is easy for one to look at the special purpose irons pictured in this category and smile or just nod one's head in agreement or appreciation of the iron designs and their uses.

Ball and egg irons were used to smooth the inside of caps, puffy sleeves, shoulders, bustles and other curved and puffy clothing parts. Sleeve irons were used for smoothing flounces and sleeves and are usually pointed in front or have a long slender handle. Hat irons are odd shaped since they conform to the shapes of hats and hat brims with their unusual curls and curves. A tolliker is a hat iron that shapes the brim while a shackle is a hat iron that has a movable flange which was regulated to curl the outer edge of the brim. Polishing irons were used to produce a shiny glaze or gloss on starched shirts, collars and cuffs, as well as other clothing parts. Generally, polishers were smaller in size and weight compared to a normal flat iron, but it is the shape of the polisher that distinguishes it from the flat iron. Polishers have rounded edges at the front, sides and back in various combinations and often have a patterned bottom such as a diamond grid, ridges or dots. They were used in many European countries but in America polishers were quite numerous. Seam irons were used to smooth narrow seam areas, hence, the design of the narrow iron body. Billiard table irons maintained a smooth felt on a pool or billiard table. The beveled sides of the iron meshed with the taper of the billiard table. Other special purpose irons pictured in this section include a button hole iron, pants seam presses, tie presses and flower irons used to imprint designs into fabrics.

Collector Hints

This category of irons shows much variety and novelty in design and can provide the collector with many possible subjects for collecting. Ball and egg irons are common in Europe and are found in a wide variety of sizes and shapes. The more desirable ball, egg or mushroom irons have holding stands of cast iron or other special holders. Hat irons and flower irons are all so different and are fun to collect. There are numerous styles of polishers and new variations show up frequently.

Look for well marked items (names, patent dates, etc.) and unusual shapes and bottom surfaces. Many polishers, ball irons and other special purpose irons are readily available and prices of the more common examples are still very reasonable. No reproductions are known at this time.

203 (L) Leather Press, Dutch, bootmaker's press with slide door for slug, very massive, late 1800, L 20", R5, V12 (Carson)
(R) Plaiter, **NORTH BROS MFG CO, CROWN PLAITER, PHILADA**, stenciling on black surfaces, other surfaces chromed, late 1800, L 10", R5, V11 (Carson)

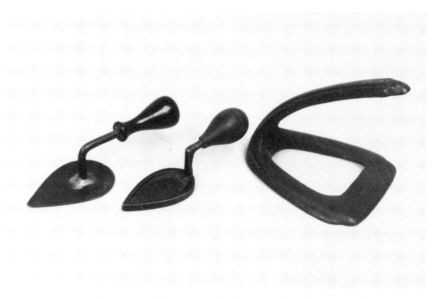

204 (L) Edge/Seam, European, for delicate pressing jobs, thin base, late 1800, L 5 1/2", R3, V7
(M) Edge/Seam, like **(L)**, brass base with recessed center, late 1800, L 4 3/4", R3, V8
(R) Button Hole, open center section to press around buttons, late 1800, L 4 1/2", R5, V10 (J. Irons)

205 (L) Velvet Polisher, French, speciality stand with French flat iron, used to press the underside of velvet by pulling material over iron, late 1800, L 14", R4, V8
(R) Polisher, round bottom, iron cannot rest upright on bottom, late 1800, L 6", R4, V7

206 (L) Button Hole, **PAT JUNE 1901, IRON ___ TOY**, removable handle, slot for ironing around buttons, L 6 1/2", R5, V9 (Hopmeyer)
(R) Slug Polisher, European, curved front, leather handle, mid 1800, L 5", R5, V10 (Hopmeyer)

207 (L) Reversible, **NOBLE IRON CO, PAT'D 1893, NEWARK NJ**, removable handle, 2 smoothing surfaces, 1 is ³/₄" wide, L 5 ¹/₈", R5, V10 (Herrick)
(R) Embossing Combination, **MYERS, PAT MAR 1873**, Frederick Myers from New York, detachable plates with designs, L 5 ⁷/₈", R5, V12 (Herrick)

208 (L) Vertical Polisher, brass handle, late 1800, L 5 ³/₈", R3, V8
(R) Vertical Polisher, wood handle, ¹/₂" thick base thins toward edge, late 1800, L 5 ³/₈", R3, V8

209 (L) Sleeve, **PAT'D JUNE 15 1897 ("C" in shield)**, long flat toe, L 9 ⁷/₈", R4, V8 (Balestri)
(M) Sleeve, **ASBESTOS SAD IRON, PAT MAY 22ND 1900**, long toe, L 7 ³/₄", R3, V8 (Balestri)
(R) Sleeve, **GENEVA ILL**, by W. H. Howell Co, thick toe, late 1800, L 6 ³/₄", R3, V7 (Balestri)

210 (L) Sleeve, **ASBESTOS SAD IRON, PAT MAY 22ND 1900**, with original box, **ASBESTOS FLOUNCE IRON, No. 50, DOVER MFG CO, ASBESTOS LINED**, L 6 ³/₄", R1, V4 (no box), R4, V8 (with box)
(R) Sleeve, **GUELPH WAP** overlaid letters, late 1800, L 7", R3, V6

211 (L) Sleeve, late 1800, L 6", R1, V4
(M) Sleeve, **HUB**, late 1800, L 5 7/8", R2, V5
(R) Sleeve, **B & D 1 (star)**, Bless & Drake, Newark, NJ, late 1800, L 6 7/8", R1, V4

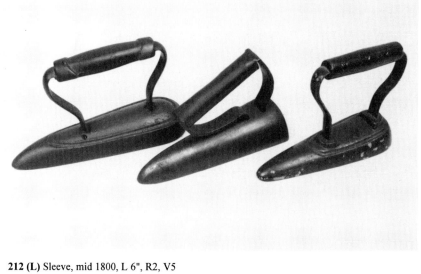

212 (L) Sleeve, mid 1800, L 6", R2, V5
(M) Sleeve, English, mid 1800, L 6 1/4", R3, V6
(R) Sleeve, pat. on July 14, 1863 by Nathaniel Waterman, Boston, MA, L 6", R2, V5

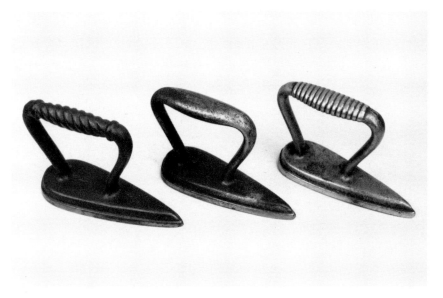

213 (L) Sleeve, all cast, rope twist handle, late 1800, L 5 3/8", R1, V4
(M) Sleeve, all cast, plain handle, late 1800, L 5 1/4", R1, V4
(R) Sleeve, all cast, rib handle, late 1800, L 5 1/4", R1, V4

214 (L) Sleeve, **#12 (shield with "C")**, Colebrookdale of Pottstown, PA, mid 1800, L 7 3/4", R1, V4
(R) Sleeve, **#8**, like **(L)**, L 6 7/8", R1, V4

215 (L) Sleeve, **SHERMAN'S IMPROVED**, mid 1800, L 6 ¹/8", R3, V7 (Carson)
(R) Sleeve, **HARPER, CHICAGO, PAT AUG 27, 07**, removable handle, L 6 ¹/4", R3, V8 (Carson)

216 (L) Sleeve, **#376** at point, late 1800, L 8 ¹/2", R1, V4
(R) Sleeve, **GRAND UNION TEA COMPANY**, Scranton, PA, 1870's, L 7 ⁷/8", R1, V4

217 (L) Sleeve, No. 1, **SENSIBLE, MADE IN USA**, N. R. Streeter, Groton, NY, PAT **SEPT 6 1887** on handle, L 6 ⁷/8", R1, V4
(M) Sleeve, **SENSIBLE, No. 5**, like **(L)**, L 8", R1, V4
(R) Sleeve, **SENSIBLE, No. 1**, like **(L)**, L 6 ⁷/8", R1, V4

218 (L) Sleeve, Mt. Joy type handle, late 1800, L 6 ³/8", R3, V7 (Carson)
(R) Sleeve, **PLUTO, THE CUTLER-HAMMER MFG CO, MILWAUKEE, PAT'D MAY 7 '07**, electric with removable handle, L 7", R4, V9 (Carson)

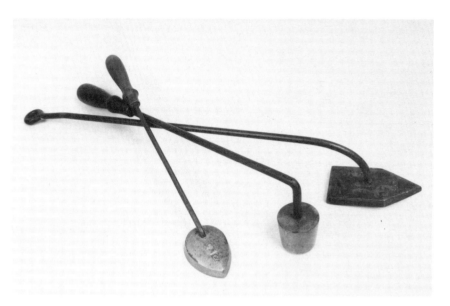

219 (L) Sleeve, **THE OBER MFG CO, CHAGRIN FALLS O, 801**, late 1800, L 6 ³/₄", R2, V6
(R) Sleeve, **G.H. OBER, CHAGRIN FALLS O, PAT MAY 28 '95**, handle **PATENTED JULY 21 1894**, L 7 ³/₄", R2, V6

220 (L) Long Sleeve, **#3 (shield "C")**, Colebrookdale, Pottstown, PA, late 1800, L 15 ⁵/₈", R3, V8
(M) Long Sleeve, European, truncated cone shape, late 1800, L 18 ¹/₄", R4, V8
(R) Long Sleeve, French, wrought iron, mid 1800, L 25", R3, V8 (Carson)

221 (F) Long Sleeve, French, late 1800, L 19", R4, V8 (Holtzman)
(M) Long Sleeve, French, late 1800, L 13 ¹/₂", R4, V8 (Holtzman)
(B) Long Sleeve, French, flower design, late 1800, L 15", R4, V8 (Holtzman)

222 (L) Hat, **R RAINES & CO, S BRUSHFIELD**, wood tolliker, different grooves on all 4 sides, late 1800, L 3 ³/₈", R3, V7 (Carson)
(M) Hat, wood tolliker, late 1800, L 5 ³/₄", R3, V7
(R) Hat, **JBS CO**, wood tolliker, late 1800, L 5", R3, V7

223 (L) Hat, tolliker, solid cast with typical wood handle, curved side, late 1800, L 4", R3, V7

(M) Hat, shackle, one groove in bottom, angled side, lead weighted top, late 1800, L 3 $^{1}/_{8}$", R3, V8

(R) Hat, shackle, angled bottom edge is brass, late 1800, L 3 $^{1}/_{2}$", R3, V8

224 (L) Hat, tolliker, **M. CO**, smooth bottom, early 1900, L 5 $^{1}/_{2}$", R3, V8
(R) Hat, shackle, early 1900, L 3", R3, V7

225 (L) Hat, tolliker, **AHS CO NY**, flat bottom, curved side, wood handle, late 1800, L 4", R3, V8

(R) Hat, tolliker, 2 curved opposing grooves in bottom, wood handle, late 1800, L 3 $^{1}/_{2}$", R3, V8

226 (L) Hat, **McCOYS PAT PD**, arched cutout in bottom, left side of bottom smaller than right, slight taper to bottom, late 1800, L 4 $^{3}/_{4}$", R4, V8
(R) Hat, **McCOYS PAT PEND**, like (L) but with different handle, late 1800, L 4 $^{3}/_{4}$", R4, V8

227 (L) Hat, steam heated, curved sides, with rounded edges, insulated top, late 1800, L 5 1/2", R3, V7
(R) Hat, tolliker, flat bottom with 2 arched flaired grooves, late 1800, L 5 1/4", R3, V7

228 (L) Hat, shackle, iron, flat bottom, late 1800, L 5 1/8", R3, V7
(M) Hat, shackle, like **(L)**, early 1900, L 3 1/2", R3, V7
(R) Hat, tolliker, solid base, curved sides, flat bottom, early 1900, L 4 1/8", R3, V7

229 (L) Hat, tolliker, all cast iron, arched bottom, late 1800, L 4 3/4", R3, V8
(R) Hat, tolliker, wave-like bottom, late 1800, L 4 1/2", R3, V8

230 (L) Hat, tolliker, French, all cast, smooth bottom, beveled sides, late 1800, L 5 1/4", R3, V7
(R) Polisher, French, **6**, rounded back, late 1800, L 6 5/8", R3, V7

231 (L) Hat, English, **SCHADLER, No. 5471, PATENT,** heated with hot water, curved base, early 1900, L 4 ^{1}/$_2$", R4, V9 (Balestri)
(R) Polisher, **LAUNDRY POLISH IRON, 1852,** detachable slip-out handle, L 5", R4, V8 (Balestri)

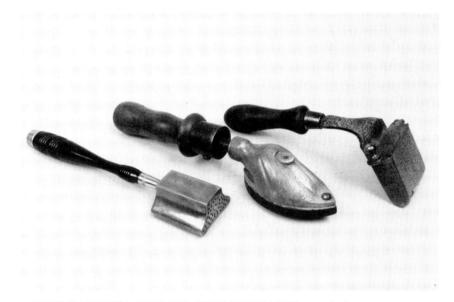

232 (L) Hat, **PAT USA, ENGLAND, GERMANY, FRANCE,** rotary hat iron pat. by Alexander McDonald, Brooklyn, NY, June 7, 1892, heated on gas jet, head rotates, L 9 ^{1}/$_2$", R3, V7
(M) Bootmaker's, electric, Dutch, early 1900, L 10 ^{1}/$_2$", R4, V8
(R) Hat, European, slug, iron with latch, late 1800, L 8 ^{1}/$_2$", R3, V8

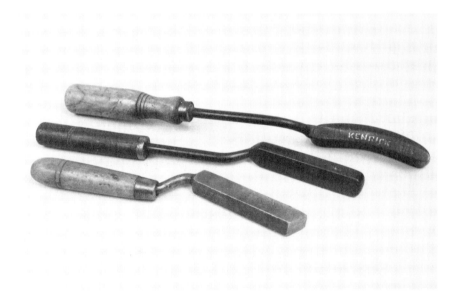

233 (L) Hat, **WM JOHNSON INC, NEWARK NJ, USA,** about 1900, L 9 ^{1}/$_2$", R3, V7
(M) Hat, European, about 1900, L 13", R3, V7
(R) Hat, English, **KENRICK No. 1,** about 1900, L 15", R3, V7

234 (L) Hat, shackle, both sides movable, about 1925, L 3 ^{3}/$_4$", R4, V9 (Baumunk)
(R) Hat, **VAC 7 ^{3}/$_8$", M.A. CUMING & CO, NY, 2 47,** 2 pcs for crown of hat, tin top, wood bottom, about 1925, L 7", R5, V10 (Sinclair)

235 (L) Hat, electric hat press with adjustable size indicator, early 1900, L 16", R3, V7
(R) Machine, burnisher, **ENTREKIN'S SWING-BACK BURNISHER, PAT'D DEC 2 73, MAR 25 79, JAN 11 87**, pinstriped in yellow, red and blue over black, with tin alcohol heater, L 16", R5, V11 (Carson)

236 (L) Hat, **8**, slug iron that was converted to steam, early 1900, L 7 1/2", R3, V5
(M) Hat, **DORAN BROTHERS, DANBURY CONN, PAT FEB 6 06, AUG 17 15**, electric, L 7 1/4", R3, V6
(R) Hat, **C. S. ANDREWS, DANBURY CT, 3**, leather wrapped handle, slug with sliding door, late 1800, L 7", R3, V9

237 (L) Hat, hollow body, wood handle, early 1900, L 6 3/4", R3, V7
(R) Hat, solid iron, late 1800, L 7 3/8", R3, V5

238 (L) Hat, **WAW 3**, slug with sliding door, late 1800, L 7", R3, V6
(M) Hat, **J. MOONN, 14, PHILA**, slug with sliding door, late 1800, L 6 3/8", R3, V7
(R) Hat, **MAHONY, 8**, slug with sliding door, late 1800, L 6 3/4", R3, V7

239 (L) Seam, **THE LIGHTNING, THE WELLER, PAT FEB 9 '92, BRIDGEPORT CT USA**, L 7", R4, V9 (Holtzman)
(R) Doily Press, European, all brass, late 1800, L 5 ¹/₈", R4, V9 (Holtzman)

240 (L) Seam, **H. S. ELWES, SPRINGFIELD O**, late 1800, L 7 ¹/₂", Width 1 ³/₄", R4, V8
(R) Seam, brass handle, L 7 ³/₄", Width 1 ¹/₈", R4, V8

241 (L) Seam, **PAT APD FOR**, handle opens up and folds back out of heat, late 1800, L 6 ³/₄", Width 1 ¹/₄", R4, V9
(R) Seam, handle opens, late 1800, L 7", Width 1 ¹/₄", R4, V9

242 (L) Polisher, **PATENT JULY 14 63**, **No. 1**, egg shaped, L 4 ¹/₂", R4, V8
(M) Seam, **JAMES SEAM IRON**, solid cast iron, mid 1800, L 6", R5, V10 (Carson)
(R) Polisher, odd form, late 1800, L 7", R4, V9

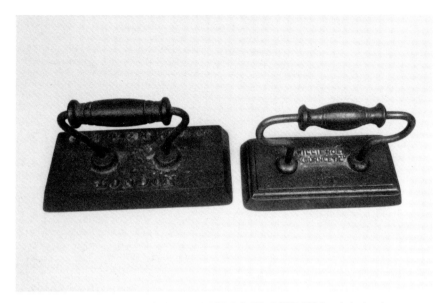

243 (L) Billiard Table, English, **GEO. WRIGHT & CO, LONDON**, beveled edge, late 1800, L 10", R3, V7
(R) Billiard Table, English, **WILLIE HOLT BURNLEY LTD**, beveled edge, late 1800, L 8 ³/₄", R3, V7

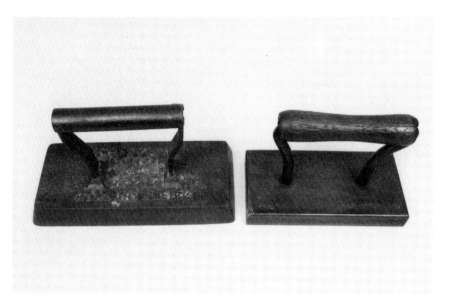

244 (L) Billiard Table, English, **WM. SYKES BILLARD TABLE HAKOR, JORBURY & LEEDS**, beveled edges, mid 1800, L 10", R3, V7
(R) Doily/Billiard Table, English, no beveled edge, mid 1800, L 8", R3, V7 (Carson)

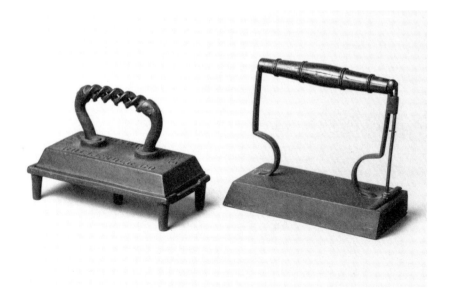

245 (L) Billiard Table, English, **THE BRUNSWICK BLAKE COLLENDER CO**, twisted handle, late 1800, L 9 ¹/₂", R3, V8 (Hopmeyer)
(R) Billiard Table, slug, English, lift-up gate, mid 1800, L 11 ¹/₂", R5, V12 (Hopmeyer)

246 (L) Standing Egg, English, **A. K. & SON No. 1**, mid 1800, Egg 2 ³/₄", R4, V8
(M) Standing Egg, English, flat underside, mid 1800, Egg 5", R4, V9
(R) Standing Egg, English, massive piece, mid 1800, Egg 4 ¹/₂", R4, V9 (Carson)

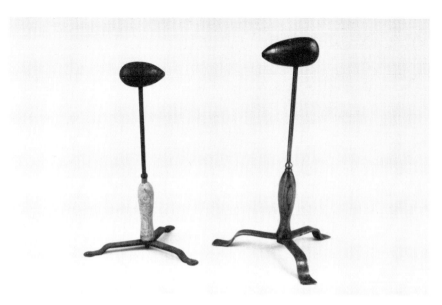

247 **(L)** Standing Egg, French, about 1900, Ht 12 ³/4", R3, V8
(R) Standing Egg, French, late 1800, Ht 14 ¹/2", R3, V8 (Carson)

248 **(L)** Standing Egg, European, fancy cast base, mid 1800, Egg 4 ¹/2", R4, V9
(R) Standing Ball, European, fancy cast base, Ball ³/4" dia, R4, V9

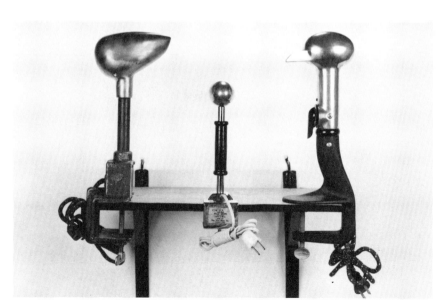

249 **(L)** Egg, electric, **ELECTRICAL PUFF IRON BY GRAND MFG CO, LOS ANGELES, CALIF**, pat. 1933, Ht 11", R4, V10 (Balestri)
(M) Ball, electic, **VIN MAX TRADEMARK PUFF IRON BY VIN MAX CO, OAKLAND CALIF**, about 1950, Ht 7 ³/4", R3, V9 (Balestri)
(R) Ball, electric, ball the shape of a bird head, mid 1900, Ht 11", R4, V10 (Balestri)

250 **(L)** Electric Mounting Iron, **MAJESTIC MOUNTING IRON, EASTMAN KODAK CO, ROCHESTER NY**, rectangular base with small point, about 1900, L 6 ¹/4", R5, V9 (McClure)
(R) Egg, **G & BM CO**, with companion trivet, late 1800, Egg 2 ¹/2", R5, V9 (McClure)

83

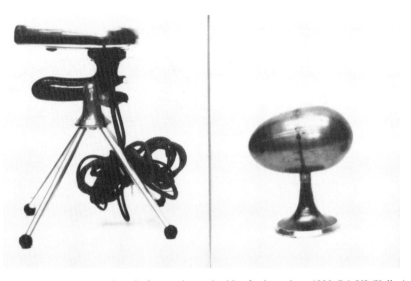

251 (L) Electric Standing Egg, **THERMA**, early 1900, Egg 5 $^3/_4$", R3, V7
(M) Electric Standing Egg, wood base and handle with threaded interchangeable top, early 1900, Top 3 $^1/_4$", R4, V8
(R) Standing Egg, base held 3 irons, early 1900, Egg 4 $^1/_2$", R3, V7

252 (L) Velvet Steam, French, for pressing underside of velvet, about 1930, R4, V9 (Kelley)
(R) Egg, French, late 1800, L 5", R4, V9 (Kelley)

253 (L-1) Ball, European, late 1800, Ball 1" dia, R2, V6
(L-2) Ball, like **(L-1)**, Ball $^7/_8$" dia, R2, V6
(L-3) Ball, like **(L-1)**, Ball 2" dia, R3, V7
(L-4) Ball, like **(L-1)**, Ball 1 $^3/_8$" dia, R3, V7
(L-5) Mushroom, European, late 1800, Top 3 $^1/_2$" dia, R3, V8
(L-6) Mushroom, English, all brass, mid 1800, Top 2 $^1/_2$" dia, R4, V8

254 (L) Egg, European, cast egg on rod with iron handle, late 1800, Egg 2 $^1/_4$", R2, V6
(M) Egg, like **(L)**, wood handle, Egg 2", R2, V6

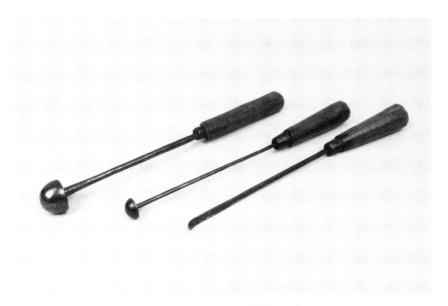

255 (L) Mushroom, European, mid 1800, L 10", R3, V6 (Carson)
(M) Mushroom, European, mid 1800, L 10 ¹/₂", R3, V6 (Carson)
(R) Deer Feet, European, used with flower iron, mid 1800, L 10 ¹/₄", R4, V7 (Carson)

256 (L-1) Flower, brass top/base, late 1800, L 7 ¹/₂", R3, V7
(L-2) Flower, **G. MOLLAS, NY**, brass base, iron top, late 1800, L 7 ¹/₄", R3, V7
(L-3) Flower, brass top/base, late 1800, L 8", R3, V7
(L-4) Flower, brass base, iron top, late 1800, L 7 ¹/₄", R3, V7

257 (L-1) Flower, **G. MOLLA, NY**, brass base, iron top, late 1800, L 6 ³/₄", R3, V7
(L-2) Flower, **G. MOLLA, NY**, brass base, iron top, late 1800, L 8 ¹/₄", R3, V7
(L-3) Flower, **G. MOLLA, NY**, brass base, iron top, late 1800, L 7 ¹/₄", R3, V7
(L-4) Flower, **A. F. TOOL CO, NY**, brass top/base, late 1800, L 6 ¹/₄", R3, V7

258 (L-1) Flower, **J. ALENTE, NY**, brass top, iron base, late 1800, L 9 ¹/₂", R3, V8
(L-2) Flower, brass top/base, late 1800, L 7", R3, V8
(L-3) Flower, **G. MOLLA**, iron top only, late 1800, L 8", R3, V8 (complete)
(L-4) Flower, brass top only, late 1800, L 8 ³/₄", R3, V7 (complete)

259 (F) Glove Form, **PAT'D MAY 1, 83**, brass thumb, L 11 3/8", R4, V10 (Baumunk)
(L) Ball, English, grooved cast base, late 1800, Ht 13 1/2", R4, V9 (Baumunk)
(R) Electric Egg, French, **BABETH, 220 VOLTS**, about 1980, Ht 10", R2, V8 (Baumunk)

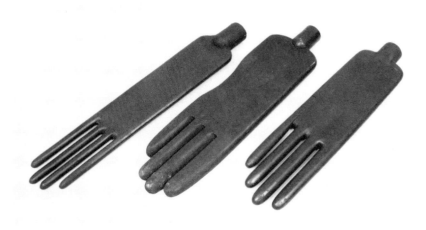

260 (L) Glove Form, steam heated glove press, cast iron, late 1800, L 15 1/2", R4, V9
(M) Glove Form, steam heated, cast brass, late 1800, L 14 3/4", R4, V9
(R) Glove Form, like **(L)**, L 14", R4, V9

261 (L) Polisher, French, **REPOSE, No. 2,** (**anchor** with **CF**), ridged bottom parallel to back edge, late 1800, L 6 3/4", R4, V8
(M) Polisher, French, bottom design for **(R)**
(R) Polisher, French, **BREVETE SG DG**, (**anchor** with **CF**), grid bottom like **(M)**, late 1800, L 6 1/2", R4, V8 (Carson)

262 (L) Electric Hand Polisher, vertical grip position, early 1900, L 7 1/2", R3, V8 (Holtzman)
(M) Polisher, French, very coarse bottom grid, grid pyramidal, late 1800, L 6 1/4", R4, V9 (Holtzman)
(R) Electric Hat, tolliker, curved side, groove in base, early 1900, L 4 3/4", R4, V8 (Holtzman)

263 (L) Polisher, **(star)**, 2 piece iron, clip-on shoe-like base, smooth bottom, late 1800, L 6", R4, V9

(R) Polisher, **ELECTRIC, PAT JULY 15 1890, REISSUED OCT 7 79, JUNE 6 80**, transverse grooves on bottom in middle portion only, removable handle, L 6", R4, V9

264 (L) Polisher, **MRS STREETERS, #2, GEM POLISHER, PAT SEPT 6 87**, removable handle, front is flat angled surface, L 5 ½", R4, V8

(R) Polisher, **GEM**, slug heated, top lifts off, front is a flat angled surface, late 1800, L 5", R4, V9

265 (L) Polisher, large size polisher with checkered bottom, late 1800, L 5 ³/4", R3, V7 (Holtzman)

(R) Polisher, **SWEENEY IRON, PAT NOV 17 96, #4, MFG BY BAIRD & CO, PITTSBURGH PA**, pat. by Mary Sweeney, L 7", R4, V8 (Holtzman)

266 (L) Polisher, **G.S. & CO, IXL POLISH, 8**, rounded edges, late 1800, L 5 ½", R4, V7 (Carson)

(R) Polisher, **GLOSSING AND FLUTING IRON, PATENT**, rounded edges, fluting attachment missing, late 1800, L 6", R4, V9

267 (L) Polisher, **ENTERPRISE MFG CO OF PA, PAT OCT 1 67, JAN 16 77, PHILADELPHIA PA, 1872, STAR POLISHER**, rounded edges, L 5 ^{1}/$_2$", R1, V5
(R) Polisher, **ENTERPRISE MFG CO, PHILA, PAT OCT 1 67, PAT JAN 16 77, No. 101, GIRLS STAR PATENT, GROUND**, one point curves up, L 4 ^{7}/$_8$", R1, V5

268 (L) Polisher, English, smooth bottom, late 1800, L 3 ^{5}/$_8$", R3, V6
(M) Polisher, French, curved bottom, early 1900, L 5", R3, V6
(R) Polisher, all cast iron, rounded bottom edges, smooth bottom, late 1800, L 5", R4, V7

269 (L) Cap, French, **LT**, late 1800, L 3 ^{7}/$_8$", R2, V4
(M) Cap, English, **2, DALE CO**, late 1800, L 4 ^{1}/$_4$", R2, V4
(R) Cap, English, **SMITE, #0**, late 1800, L 4", R2, V4

270 (L) Polisher, **STAR POLISHER**, all cast with rounded edges, late 1800, L 4 ^{7}/$_8$", R4, V8
(M) Polisher, edges less rounded than **(L)**, late 1800, L 4 ^{1}/$_2$", R3, V8
(R) Polisher, **SUFFOLK POLISHER**, all cast, rounded edges, late 1800, L 4 ^{7}/$_8$", R4, V8

271 (L) Polisher, **COOKS**, like **(M)** but different handle, rounded edges, L 5", R3, V7
(M) Polisher, **MAB COOK, 1, PATD DEC 5 1848**, rounded edges, L 5 ¼", R3, V8
(R) Polisher, all cast, rounded edges, late 1800, L 4 ¾", R3, V7

272 **(L)** Polisher, slug heated, top lifts off, rounded bottom edges, late 1800, L 5 ¼", R4, V8
(R) Polisher, **HOODS PATENT, PATD JAN 15 1867**, Milford, NH, soapstone body, rounded bottom edges, L 5 ⅛", R4, V10

273 **(L)** Polisher, English, **CARRON, 2**, round bottom, late 1800, L 4 ⅝", R3, V7
(R) Polisher, English, **(Star of David)** in circle, round bottom, late 1800, L 5", R3, V7

274 **(L)** Polisher, English, **W. CROSS**, round bottom, late 1800, L 5 ¾", R3, V7
(R) Polisher, English, **No. 1, J & JS**, round bottom, early 1900, L 4 ¼", R3, V7

275 (L) Polisher, pat. by Joel Gleason, Whitestone, NY, July 12, 1870, ribbed edgework and tin heat shield, L 5", R3, V7
(R) Polisher, like **(L)** but with different handle and no heat shield, late 1800, L 5", R3, V7

276 (L) Polisher, **KEYSTONE (symbol of keystone)**, pat. by Milton Shimer, Freemansburg, PA on Sept 4, 1883, L 4 $^7/_8$", R3, V8
(R) Polisher, French, **#1**, late 1800, L 4 $^7/_8$", R2, V4

277 (L) Polisher, **GENEVA ILL, (star)**, W. H. Howell, smooth bottom, late 1800, L 5", R3, V7
(R) Polisher, **N. E. BUTT CO, PROV RI**, rope edge, smooth bottom, late 1800, L 5 $^1/_4$", R3, V7

278 (L) Polisher, **LINK & MAHONY, PATD NOV 28 1876, TROY NY**, diamond grid bottom, L 5 $^3/_4$", R4, V7 (Carson)
(R) Polisher, egg shaped, rounded back, late 1800, L 4 $^3/_4$", R3, V6

279 (FL) Hat, tolliker, **GEM**, one groove, late 1800, L 4 $^1/8$", R3, V7
(FR) Sleeve, **THE OBER MFG CO, CHAGRIN FALLS O, 80**, late 1800, L 6 $^3/4$", R3, V6
(R) Electric Polisher, **SIMPLEX QUALITY**, diamond grid bottom, late 1800, L 4 $^5/8$", R4, V7 (Borsch)

280 (L) Polisher, **THE GOELDS**, smooth bottom, late 1800, L 4 $^5/8$", R3, V4
(R) Polisher, **L J CO, ILION NY**, smooth bottom, late 1800, L 4 $^7/8$", R3, V4

281 (L) Polisher, diamond grid bottom, late 1800, L 4 $^1/2$", R2, V3
(M) Polisher, smooth bottom, late 1800, L 4 $^1/4$", R2, V3
(R) Polisher, **THE GOULDS**, checkered cylindrical handle, smooth bottom, late 1800, L 4 $^1/2$", R3, V4

282 (L) Polisher, **(Indian)** in relief, diamond grid bottom, late 1800, L 4 $^3/8$", R4, V8 (Carson)
(R) Polisher, **WAR HUNT**, diamond grid bottom, late 1800, L 4 $^3/8$", R4, V8 (Carson)

283 (L) Polisher, **MAHONY, TROY NY, PAT NOV 23 1876**, diamond grid bottom, L 4 $^{7}/_{8}$", R2, V4 (Carson)
(M) Polisher, **MAHONY, TROY NY, NOV 23 1876**, different location of marks, diamond grid bottom, L 4 $^{1}/_{4}$", R2, V4
(R) Polisher, like **(M)** but different location of marks and rough bottom, L 4 $^{1}/_{2}$", R3, V5

284 (L) Polisher, **G**, diamond grid bottom, late 1800, L 4 $^{3}/_{8}$", R2, V4
(M) Polisher, **TROY, #80**, diamond grid bottom, late 1800, L 4 $^{3}/_{8}$", R2, V4
(R) Polisher, **(spectacles)**, diamond grid bottom, late 1800, L 4 $^{1}/_{4}$", R3, V6

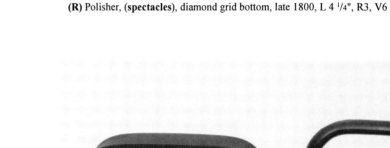

285 (L) Polisher, **MAHONY, TROY NY**, diamond grid bottom, variation of handle made in large quantity, late 1800, L 12", R1, V3
(R) Polisher, diamond grid bottom, late 1800, L 7 $^{1}/_{2}$", R2, V4

286 (L) Polisher, French, beveled sides, smooth bottom, mid 1800, L 5 $^{5}/_{8}$", R3, V5
(R) Polisher, smooth bottom, mid 1800, L 4 $^{5}/_{8}$", R3, V6

287 (L) Polisher, **L. KALLMANS SONS, 36 NORFOLK ST, NY, #6, (6 pt star)**, bird tracks for bottom pattern, late 1800, L 5 $^1/_2$", R3, V6
(R) Polisher, **QUEST**, smooth bottom, beveled sides, late 1800, L 6", R4, V7 (Carson)

288 (L) Polisher, **#8**, rough bottom, late 1800, L 6 $^3/_8$", R3, V6
(R) Polisher, **TLM CO, #7**, smooth bottom, rounded edges, late 1800, L 5 $^1/_4$", R3, V6

289 (L) Polisher, **A. J. BELLAMY, TROY NY, 7**, steep beveled sides, rough bottom, late 1800, L 6 $^1/_8$", R3, V6
(R) Polisher, **BELLAMY, TROY NY**, beveled sides, rough bottom, late 1800, L 6 $^1/_4$", R3, V6

290 (L) Polisher, **M. MAHONY, TROY NY, 6**, rough bottom, rounded back edge, late 1800, L 5 $^3/_8$", R3, V6
(R) Polisher, **MAHONY MFG CO, TROY NY**, rough bottom, late 1800, L 4 $^7/_8$", R3, V6

291 (L) Polisher, **JOS HERNBERG, TROY NY, No. 11**, areas of dots and roughness on bottom, rounded top surface edges, late 1800, L 6", R3, V7

(R) Polisher, **NOVEL FACE, W. H. HAWKS, EDGEWATER NY, PAT PENDING, #8**, beveled sides, rough bottom, late 1800, L 6 1/4", R4, V8

292 (L-1) Edge, European, round shaped, all brass, late 1800, L 8", R4, V7 (Carson)
(L-2) Edge, European, almond shaped, late 1800, L 10", R3, V7
(L-3) Edge, European, rectangular shape, late 1800, L 9", R3, V7
(L-4) Edge, **MADE IN GERMANY, PETER J. MICHELS**, teardrop shape, early 1900, L 10", R2, V7

293 (L) Pleating Scissors, single, wrought iron, early 1800, L 10 1/2", R3, V7
(M) Pleating Scissors, single, wrought iron, early 1800, L 11", R3, V7
(R) Pleating Scissors, double, wrought iron, mid 1800, L 11", R3, V7

294 (L) Fluting Scissors, wood grips, about 1900, L 9 1/4", R3, V6
(M) Fluting Scissors, wrought iron, flutes riveted to handle, early 1800, L 14 1/4", R4, V9
(R) Fluting Scissors, wrought iron, early 1800, L 12 3/4", R4, V9

FLAT IRONS

Flat irons or sad irons include all those irons that are used solely for smoothing and are constructed of cast or wrought iron. Included in this category are those irons which were designed to have cooler or cold handles - i.e., detachable wood handles, handles with holes, handles with insulation, and heat shields or other unique designs which can keep the iron handle cooler than the iron base. The greatest number of manufactured irons were flat irons. Hence, this category has the greatest number of irons available to the collector today. These are the irons that everyone's grandmother had in the kitchen and heated on the stove. Since many of the flat irons are quite common and similar in design, this book focuses primarily on the more unique designs and does not show the variation in size or design of the most common flat irons. Some foundries offered irons in graduated sizes from 0, 1, 2, 3 up to 24 or more. In reality, an entire book could be devoted to flat irons to cover all the types and sizes manufactured.

Collector Hints

Designs on the iron body and handle always enhance collectibility. Various handle styles and attachments (handle to base) provide for a wide range of collectible flat irons that are still available. Prices of flat irons are still low compared to other types of irons and only a few reproductions have appeared today, such as the blacksmith type made in Williamsburg.

295 **(L)** Cast, swan, late 1800, L 9", R5, V12 (Fingerman)
(R) Cast, Belgian, (**loving couple**), late 1800, L 6 ³/₄", R4, V9 (Fingerman)

296 **(L)** Cast, horse, European, late 1800, L 5 ³/₈", R5, V12
(R) Cast, horse, European, late 1800, L 3 ⁵/₈", R5, V12 (Holtzman)

297 (L) Cast, French, **DC #10**, late 1800, L 7 ⁷/₈", R3, V7 (Carson)
(M) Cast, French, **(loving couple)**, late 1800, L 7 ¹/₈", R4, V9 (Carson)
(R) Cast, French, **(urn with flowers)**, late 1800, L 6 ⁵/₈", R3, V8 (Carson)

298(L) Cast, French, **ANNA, (flowers and cherub)**, late 1800, L 7", R4, V9 (Holtzman)
(R) Cast, French, shaped handle, **(flowers in urn)**, late 1800, L 7", R3, V8 (Holtzman)

299 (L) Wrought, hand forged from 1 piece of iron, both ends are round, mid 1800, L 5", R4, V8 (McClure)
(R) Cast, snake handle, late 1800, L 6 ¹/₂", R5, V9 (McClure)

300 (L-1) Cast, Russian, **H3, (crossed hammers)** along the sides, late 1800, L 6 ¹/₂", R5, V9 (Marty Carson)
(L-2) Cast, Russian, **N-3 3**, late 1800, L 6 ¹/₂", R4, V7 (Marty Carson)
(L-3) Cast, Russian, **2 HIH**, late 1800, L 6 ³/₈", R4, V7 (Marty Carson)
(L-4) Cast, Russian, **2 (symbols)**, late 1800, L 5 ¹/₂", R4, V7 (Marty Carson)

301 (L) Cast, early 1900, L 6", R2, V5
(M) Cast, French, late 1800, L 6 5/8", R4, V8
(R) Cast, Mexican, **PAGOEL, HECHO EN MEXICO**, about 1930, L 5 5/8", R1, V3

302 (L) Cast, French, **SD #10**, **(wreath/flowers)**, late 1800, L 7 7/8", R3, V7
(M) Cast, French, **GL #9**, **(sun)**, late 1800, L 7 7/8", R3, V7 (Carson)
(R) Cast, French, **SIV #5**, **(4 leaf clover)**, late 1800, L 6 3/4", R2, V6 (Carson)

303 (L) Cast, French, **MC (stars) 1927**, brass handle, L 8", R4, V8
(M) Cast, French, **HL**, about 1900, L 6 7/8", R2, V5
(R) Cast, French, floral top, about 1900, L 7", R3, V7

304 (L) Cast, French, **#2**, **(anchor)**, belled out handle, late 1800, L 6 7/8", R2, V5
(M) Cast, French, **BG**, belled out handle, late 1800, L 6", R2, V4
(R) Cast, French, late 1800, L 7 1/4", R3, V7

305 (L) Cast, French, **LE GAULOIS #5**, **(warrior)**, about 1900, L 6 ¼", R3, V6
(M) Cast, French, **LE CAIFFA No. 5**, **(man at table)**, about 1900, L 6 ½", R3, V6
(R) Cast, French, **JARDINIER No. 5**, **(flowers)**, about 1900, L 6 ½", R2, V5

306 (L-1) Cast, English, **SILVESTER'S PATENT SALTER**, **(pretzel)**, about 1900, L 6 ⅛", R2, V5
(L-2) Cast, English, **SERVICE BRAND**, about 1900, L 5 ⅝", R2, V5 (Carson)
(L-3) Cast, English, **CANNON, 1900, #4**, about 1900, L 5 ¼", R2, V5 (Carson)
(L-4) Cast, English, **E PUCH & CO, WEDNESBURY**, about 1900, L 5 ⅝", R2, V5 (Carson)

307 (L-1) Cast, French, **SB #17**, early 1900, L 6 ⅝", R1, V2
(L-2) Cast, French, **DARRAS, PARIS, No. 3**, late 1800, L 6 ⅞", R2, V4
(L-3) Cast, French, **16**, early 1900, L 6 ⅜", R1, V2
(L-4) Cast, French, **(horseshoe)**, early 1900, L 6", R2, V3

308 (L) Cast, **LORING PATENT, 1880 #10**, L 7", R3, V6
(M) Cast, late 1800, L 6 ⅞", R2, V4
(R) Cast, French, early 1900, L 6", R2, V3

309 (L-1) Cast, European, with companion trivet, late 1800, L 6 ³/₈", R3, V7
(L-2) Cast, French, **DG #7**, about 1900, L 7 ¹/₄", R1, V2
(L-3) Cast, European, late 1800, L 6 ³/₄", R3, V5 (Carson)
(L-4) Cast, European, late 1800, L 6 ¹/₈", R2, V4

310 (L) Cast, double pointed, late 1800, L 9", R3, V8 (Holtzman)
(R) Cast, **#7**, **(keystone)**, double pointed, late 1800, L 8 ¹/₂", R3, V8 (Holtzman)

311 (L) Cast, European, brass, stylish handle, late 1800, L 2", R4, V8 (Hopmeyer)
(R) Cast, like **(L)**, L 6 ⁵/₈", R2, V8 (Hopmeyer)

312 (FL) Cast, **WAPAK #4**, about 1900, L 5 ¹/₈", R1, V2
(FR) Cast, **STEEL #5, PAT AP'D FOR**, about 1900, L 5 ¹/₈", R4, V6
(RL) Cast, **RK & CO #9, PAT JULY 31 '66**, L 6 ³/₄", R3, V5
(RR) Cast, **POTTSTOWN #7**, late 1800, L 6 ¹/₄", R1, V2

313 (L-1) Wrought, handle forged with base, mid 1800, L 6 ³/4", R3, V7
(L-2) Wrought, handle forged with base, mid 1800, L 6 ¹/2", R3, V7
(L-3) Wrought, Mexican, bell in handle, late 1800, L 5 ¹/2", R2, V5
(L-4) Wrought, French, late 1800, L 6 ¹/4", R2, V5

314 (L) Cast, **OBER #6, PAT MAR 19 '12**, L 6", R3, V6
(M) Cast, **W #7**, about 1900, L 6 ¹/4", R1, V2
(R) Cast, **W #4**, about 1900, L 6 ³/8", R2, V3

315 (L-1) Cast, (anchor), late 1800, L 6", R2, V3
(L-2) Cast, **IXL #6**, late 1800, L 5 ³/4", R2, V2
(L-3) Cast, (anchor), #7, late 1800, L 6 ¹/8", R2, V3
(L-4) Cast, (**anchor** on handle), #6, about 1900, L 5 ³/4", R1, V2

316 (L-1) Cast, **J. SMART, BROOKLYN NY, #9**, late 1800, L 7", R3, V5
(L-2) Cast, **#7**, about 1900, L 6", R1, V2
(L-3) Cast, **RFP #6**, about 1900, L 5 ⁷/8", R2, V3
(L-4) Cast, **8**, dolphin posts, L 6", R3, V4

317 (L-1) Cast, late 1800, L 8 $^1/_8$", R3, V7 (Carson)
(L-2) Cast, (**keystone**) **#5**, late 1800, L 7 $^5/_8$", R3, V7
(L-3) Cast, brass handle, late 1800, L 6 $^5/_8$", R3, V6
(L-4) Cast, French, late 1800, L 6 $^3/_4$", R3, V7 (Carson)

318 (L) Cast, **#5**, decorated handle and sides, late 1800, L 5", R2, V4
(M) Cast, **OBER**, late 1800, L 4 $^1/_2$", R3, V6 (Carson)
(R) Cast, European, (**rose in high relief**), **V-A**, late 1800, L 4 $^3/_4$", R3, V5

319 (L-1) Cast, **#6**, late 1800, L 6", R1, V2
(L-2) Cast, **HOLLY MFG CO, LOCKPORT NY, #6**, late 1800, L 6", R2, V3
(L-3) Cast, **GENESEE VALLEY #9**, (**stars**), late 1800, L 7", R2, V2
(L-4) Cast, (**C in shield**), **#5**, Colebrookdale, late 1800, L 5 $^1/_8$", R1, V2

320 (L) Cast, European, early 1900, L 7", R1, V2
(M) Cast, **CROWN #2, PAT APP'D FOR**, late 1800, L 6 $^1/_2$", R3, V5
(R) Cast, about 1900, L 6 $^3/_4$", R2, V4

321 (L-1) Cast, Canadian, **J. SMART MFG CO, ROCKVILLE ONT, #5**, about 1900, L 5 ¹/₂", R3, V3

(L-2) Cast, **HB & CO, READING PA, #5**, about 1900, L 5 ¹/₄", R2, V2

(L-3) Cast, **PERFECTION #6**, about 1900, L 5 ¹/₂", R2, V2

(L-4) Cast, Canadian, **BS & M CO, HAMILTON**, about1900, L 5 ¹/₄", R2, V3

322 (L-1) Cast, handle altered by blacksmith, late 1800, L 5 ⁵/₈", R1, V2

(L-2) Cast, like **(L-1)**, L 4 ¹/₈", R1, V2

(L-3) Cast, lead added to make heavier, late 1800, L 4 ⁵/₈", R4, V3

(L-4) Cast, late 1800, L 5", R3, V4

(L-5) Cast, **PATENT SAD IRON**, forged handle, late 1800, L 6 ³/₈", R3, V4

323 (L-1) Cast, **LAUNDR_SS, NEW YO_K, PAT OCT 1 '67, #5**, L 5 ¹/₂", R3, V4

(L-2) Cast, **AY HUBBELL & CO, ELMIRA NY, #7**, late 1800, L 6 ¹/₈", R3, V4

(L-3) Cast, Canadian, **IVES & ALLEN, MONTREAL, #6**, late 1800, L 5 ³/₄", R3, V4

(L-4) Cast, **DOVER STAMPING CO, BOSTON, No. 6**, late 1800, L 5 ³/₄", R3, V4

(Carson)

324 Enterprise Boxed Set of 5 Cold Handle Irons, including 3 flat, 2 polishers, 3 handles, 2 trivets, late 1800, L 18 ¹/₂", R4, V10 (Holtzman)

325 Boxed Set, **ENTERPRISE SAD IRONS, THE BEST, PHILADELPHIA PA, USA,** 3 iron bases and 1 handle, about 1900, L 11 ³/₄", R4, V9

326 (L) Cold Handle, **PW WEIDA'S, PATENT MARCH 12th 1870, PHILA. PA, No. 2,** recessed clip to lock handle, handle opens and folds back, L 7", R4, V9
(M) Cold Handle, **PW WEIDA'S, PAT 1870, PHILA. PA,** L 4 ¹/₂", R5, V12 (Holtzman)
(R) Cold Handle, like **(L)** but **No. 3,** front latch mechanism, L 7", R4, V9

327 (L) Cold Handle, **5,** folded upright made the distance longer to the handle, early 1900, L 6 ¹/₂", R4, V9 (Walker)
(R) Cold Handle, coiled upright similar to **(L),** L 6 ¹/₈", R4, V9 (Walker)

328 (L-1) Cold Handle, open cast handle, about 1900, L 6 ¹/₄", R3, V6 (Carson)
(L-2) Cold Handle, Canadian, **(maple leaf),** coiled steel handle, about 1900, L 5 ¹/₂", R3, V7
(L-3) Cold Handle, **CHATTANOOGA,** late 1800, L 5 ⁵/₈", R3, V6
(L-4) Cast, **#5, (keystone),** about 1900, L 5 ¹/₈", R1, V2

329 (L) Cold Handle, Belgian, wood handle, teardrop style, early 1900, L 7 ¼", R3, V7 (Carson)
(M) Cold Handle, like **(L)**, L 7", R3, V7
(R) Cold Handle, French, **LB 2**, late 1800, L 6 ⅞", R3, V7 (Carson)

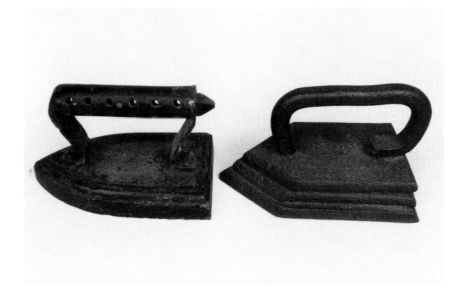

330 (L) Cold Handle, holes in handle, spike at back of handle to act as support to stand iron, late 1800, L 6 ⅛", R5, V8 (Holtzman)
(R) Hand-Made, base built-up in 3 layers, late 1800, L 6 ½", R4, V8 (Holtzman)

331 (FL) Cold Handle, **#6 (star)**, cast applied heat shield, about 1900, L 5 ¾", R5, V8
(FR) Cold Handle, **STAR IRON, ENTERPRISE MFG CO. PATENT, GROUND, PAT OCT 1 '67, #70**, L 6 ⅛", R2, V6
(RL) Cold Handle, **HOOD'S PATENT, PAT'D JAN 15 1867**, by Phineas B. Hood of Milford, NH, soapstone base insulator, 3 sizes, L 6 ⅝", R3, V9
(RR) Cold Handle, like **(FR)**, L 6 ¾", R2, V5

332 (L) Cold Handle, handle slips into iron base, late 1800, L 6", R3, V8 (Hopmeyer)
(M) Cold Handle, box, **THEO. FEWKES, PHILADELPHIA, PATENT PENDING**, heater in front of iron, two way latch to remove top and release heater, late 1800, L 8", R4, V10 (Hopmeyer)
(R) Cold Handle, sleeve, **HARPER CHICAGO NAVY**, about 1900, L 5 ⅛", R4, V9 (Hopmeyer)

333 (L) Cold Handle, **IMP. NOV 1865, #7** locking pin to attach handle, L 6 ³/₄", R4, V8 (Herrick)
(R) Cold Handle, **PAT WHC,** pat. by Peter C. Greenwalt, Aug 6, 1901, handle placed crosswise and turned, L 6 ⁷/₈", R3, V8 (Herrick)

334 (L) Cold Handle, **#3**, removable wood handle, late 1800, L 7", R4, V7 (Holtzman)
(R) Cold Handle, **TARBELL SAD IRON, COLD HANDLE #5, PAT NOV 2 1890**, L 6", R4, V8 (Holtzman)

335 (FL) Cold Handle Base, **SIMPLEX SAD IRON**, for **(RL)**, sleeve, L 7 ⁵/₈" (Borsch)
(FR) Cold Handle, **OBER #1, CHAGRIN FALLS O**, about 1900, L 6 ¹/₈", R3, V6
(RL) Cold Handle, **SIMPLEX SAD IRON**, twist latch, late 1800, L 6 ³/₈", R4, V8 (Borsch)
(RR) Cold Handle, European, **PILAKOVO**, blue porcelain, about 1900, L 7", R4, V8 (Borsch)

336 (L-1) Agate, European, **CODIN**, black/white agate surfaces, early 1900, L 7 ¹/₈", R4, V8 (Carson)
(L-2) Cold Handle, English, **EBBES, PATENT TRADE MARK, No. 5**, early 1900, L 6 ³/₈", R3, V8
(L-3) Cast, European, early 1900, L 4 ³/₄", R2, V4
(L-4) Cold Handle, European, early 1900, L 5 ¹/₈", R3, V5

337 (L-1) Cold Handle, **SENSIBLE, NRS & CO, No. 3**, pat. Sep 6, '87, L 6 ¼", R3, V7
(L-2) Cold Handle, **SENSIBLE ASBESTOS LINED, No. 90, PAT MAY 5 1908**, L 6 ½", R3, V6 without handle
(L-3) Cold Handle, **SENSIBLE ARTISAN CO, No. 8, PAT JUNE 18, 88**, L 6 ⅜", R4, V7
(L-4) Cold Handle, English, **LACE IRON, KENRICK**, about 1900, L 5 ⅛", R4, V9

338 (L) Cold Handle, **BLESS & DRAKE, NEWARK NY, PAT MAR 6 88**, L 6 ⅝", R3, V7
(M) Cold Handle, **GRISWOLD, ERIE**, late 1800, L 6 ⅝", R4, V8
(R) Cold Handle, **SIZE 2, No. 50**, metal handle, late 1800, L 6 ½", R2, V4

339 (L) Cold Handle, **WH HOWELL CO, GENEVA ILL, PAT OCT 11 05**, L 6 ½", R3, V6
(M) Cold Handle, **UNIVERSAL THERMO CELL SAD IRON, PAT JUNE 13 1911, LANDERS, FRARY & CLARK, NEW BRITAIN CONN. USA**, L 6 ⅜", R3, V7
(R) Like **(M)** but variation of handle, L 6 ⅜", R3, V7

340 (L) Cold Handle, **ROCHESTER SAD IRON**, late 1800, L 6 ⅝", R3, V6
(M) Cold Handle, **UNION, PATENTED OCT 4 1892**, L 6 ½", R3, V7
(R) Cold Handle, **GH OBER, PAT'D MAY 28, 95, SIZE 3, CHAGRIN FALLS O**, L 6 ⅛", R3, V6

341 (FL) Cold Handle, **ENTERPRISE MFG CO, PHILADELPHIA USA, No. 55**, about 1900, L 6 ³/₈", R1, V3
(FR) Cold Handle, like **(FL)**, handle variation, L 6 ³/₈", R2, V3
(RL) Cold Handle, **ENTERPRISE, PHILA USA, #92, SIZE 3**, about 1900, L 6 ³/₄", R4, V6
(RR) Cold Handle, **COLEBROOKDALE IRON CO, POTTSTOWN PA, USA**, about 1900, L 6 ³/₄", R1, V3

342(L-1) Cold Handle, slant handle, about 1900, L 7 ³/₈", R4, V8
(L-2) Cold Handle, German, **DRGM, UNIVERSAL**, handle twists and locks, knob missing, about 1900, L 6 ¹/₈", R4, V7
(L-3) Cold Handle, **CLEVELAND FOUNDRY CO, CLEVELAND O, SIZE 3, No. 60**, about 1900, L 6 ¹/₄", R3, V5
(L-4) Cold Handle, **OBER, CHAGRIN FALLS OHIO SIZE 2**, about 1900, L 6 ¹/₂", R3, V7

343 (L-1) Cold Handle, **SPECIAL HARDWARE**, about 1900, L 6 ¹/₄", R3, V6
(L-2) Cold Handle, **C (shield)**, Colebrookdale, about 1900, L 6", R1, V3
(L-3) Cold Handle, about 1900, L 6 ¹/₂", R2, V4
(L-4) Cold Handle, **HARPER #1, PAT OCT 13 '06, JULY 5 '10**, L 6", R3, V7

344 (L-1) Cold Handle, **PATENT SAD IRON**, about 1900, L 6 ¹/₈", R3, V4
(L-2) Cold Handle, **ASBESTOS SAD IRON**, about 1900, L 6 ¹/₂", R1, V3
(L-3) Cold Handle, **WEBSTERS', PAT MAY 4 1875**, L 6 ³/₈", R4, V8
(L-4) Cold Handle, **DOVER SAD IRON**, early 1900, L 6 ⁵/₈", R1, V3

LIQUID FUEL IRONS

Irons that are heated by natural gas, denatured alcohol, kerosene and gasoline are categorized as liquid fuel irons. The irons that were heated with these fuels could readily be ignited and the heat could be controlled. Since little or no smoke and soot was produced, liquid fuel irons represented a major improvement over charcoal irons.

There are specific features which characterize the various liquid fuel irons. Alcohol irons always have a wick and are clearly recognizable by the tank/wick burner assembly. The tank is non-pressurized, having a simple non-pressure threaded cap. Often the burner/tank assembly can be removed by loosening a small thumbscrew. Kerosene and gasoline irons, however, feature a pressurized fuel system. Many tanks have either a self-contained pump (Coleman type) or a special threaded fitting to attach an external pump to the tank for pressurizing. Other tanks were pressurized by the heat from the iron. Fuel tanks for kerosene/gasoline irons are constructed of heavy metal and are well manufactured compared to the thin sheet metal alcohol tanks. Kerosene/gasoline irons also have needle valves in the feed piping to the burner to control the amount of atomized fuel and hence, the temperature.

There are two basic types of natural gas irons: (1) those that have a fixed internal burner assembly and external piping for the gas and (2) those that have no burner assembly and are heated on a separate natural gas jet or burner. The latter has a hollow body with an open back or special opening which is coupled with the separate heating unit. The European models that were heated on a gas jet are generally the ox tongue slug iron type which have vent holes in the front. A possible dual heat source for some of the European irons is suggested since these European irons with front vents may also have a gate in the back to hold a slug.

Collector Hints

Liquid fuel irons are readily found and prices are still reasonable. The odd colored Coleman irons (green, red and turquoise) and other liquid fuel irons with colored porcelain are very desirable. Look for odd shaped tanks and odd locations of the tank on the iron, especially those with the tank in the handle. Original packaging with user directions add to the collectibility and value. No reproductions are known to exist.

345 Alcohol, **E.B. COSBY, PAT OCT 23 88, DEC 17 89**, wonderful and exciting form for a liquid fuel iron, sole removable to expose burner, fill pipe at front for engine body tank, Ht 7 ³/₄", L 8", R5, V12 (Furnish)

346 (L) Alcohol, revolving, **PAT MAY 4 1875**, Crocker & Farnsworth, Buffalo, NY, L 7 ¹/₄", R5, V11 (Holtzman)
(R) Alcohol, revolving, **ELLISON BRO, PHILADA, PAT JULY 6 1888**, handle is the fuel tank, L 7", R5, V11 (Holtzman)

347 (L-1) Alcohol, **GEO. L. MARION MFG CO, 129-131 FRONT ST, NEW YORK**, from Feldmeyer pat. in Germany, Apr 20 1897, with companion trivet, L 6", R3, V8
(L-2) Alcohol, German, Feldmeyer style, early 1900, no tank or burner, L 5 ³/₄", R3, V7
(L-3) Alcohol, like **(L-2)**, with companion trivet, L 5", R3, V8
(L-4) Alcohol, like **(L-2)**, L 5 ¹/₈", R3, V8

348 (L) Alcohol, **MANNING BOWMAN & CO, MERIDEN CONN, USA**, tank missing, about 1900, L 7 ¹/₄", R3, V8
(M) Alcohol, German, **G.M.T. & BRO, NY, GERMANY**, tank missing, about 1900, L 7 ¹/₄", R3, V8
(R) Alcohol, German, **MATADOR**, with companion trivet having a sun face, about 1900, L 7 ¹/₂", R4, V9

349 (L) Alcohol, revolving, pat. by Jerome R. Tarbox, May 10, 1863, Wyoming, PA, handle is fuel tank, L 6 ³/₄", R5, V12 (Fingerman)
(R) Gasoline, **STANDARD GAS IRON**, early 1900, L 7 ¹/₄", R4, V8 (Fingerman)

350 (L) Alcohol, ox tongue, European, tank missing, early 1900, L 8 ³/₈", R3, V7
(R) Alcohol, German, **BERGMANN, PAT BREV S.G.D.G.** , early 1900, L 7", R4, V8

351 (L) Alcohol, travel iron, German, burner, iron and case are all nickel plated, early 1900, L 4", R3, V7
(R) Alcohol, German, **GMT BRO, NY, GERMANY**, in original boxes for iron and burner, late 1800, L 5 ¹/₄", R5, V10

352 (L) Alcohol Travel Set, **PAT APL'D FOR**, box holds iron base, alcohol tank, burner, handle and stand, about 1900, Box L 9 ¹/₄", R5, V9 (McClure)
(R) Alcohol, **ALCOMATIC IRON, HAMILTON OHIO, PAT. AUG 28 1923**, two burners with separate valves, rear spring latch, L 7 ¹/₂", R4, V9 (McClure)

353 (L) Alcohol, **ALCOHOL GAS TWIN BURNER SAFETY IRON, PAT. FEB 16 1915, AUG 28 1923**, top slides off, L 7 ¹/₂", R4, V9 (Balestri)
(M) Gasoline, **ACORN BRASS MFG CO, CHICAGO ILL, USA, PATENTED MAY 13th 1913**, tank in handle, L 6 ⁷/₈", R5, V10 (Balestri)
(R) Kerosene, Irish, **TILLEY MODEL DN, MADE IN UK**, Tilley Lamp Co. Ltd, Dunmurry, Belfast, N. Ireland, black bakelite, about 1950, L 7 ¹/₂", R4, V8 (Balestri)

354 (L) Gasoline, **REX - PATENT**, looks like charcoal iron, early 1900, L 10", R4, V10 (Baumunk)
(M) Gasoline, **AMERICAN GAS MACHINE CO, PATENT NOV 5 1912, ALBERT LEA, MINN**, side tank, L 7 ¹/₈", R3, V9 (Baumunk)
(R) Natural Gas, English, **J. KEITH & CLACKMAN CO LTD, BRITISH PATENT 360555**, blue porcelain, early 1900, L 7 ¹/₄", R3, V8 (Baumunk)

355 (L-1) Meta Fuel, English, **BRITISH BOUDOIR IRON**, fuel container swings out from handle, early 1900, L 5 ¹/₄", R3, V6
(L-2) Meta Fuel, European, fuel held under handle, early 1900, L 5 ¹/₂", R2, V6
(L-3) Meta Fuel, Austrian, **BURGOLETTE**, white china handle, early 1900, L 5 ¹/₂", R3, V6
(L-4) Gas Jet, **PATENT JULY 4 1893**, Sultana Toilet Iron, pat. by Herbert Clayton, NYC, L 4 ¹/₂", R4, V9

356 (L) Gasoline, side tank, early 1900, L 11 ¹/₄", R4, V9 (Balestri)
(R) Gasoline, called the "Lamb", top lifts off, early 1900, L 6 ¹/₂", R4, V9 (Balestri)

357 (L) Gasoline, **WIZARD, PAT APLD FOR, TRADE MARK**, early 1900, L 6 ¼", R4, V9 (Baumunk)
(M) Meta Fuel, English, **BRITISH, BOUDOIR IRON - PATENT BCM/WS4C**, flame heats upper surface, body revolves, early 1900, L 5 ¼", R3, V8 (Baumunk)
(R) Gasoline, **NEW LEADER - PAT AUG 14 '94**, iron lays on side to fill tank, with companion trivet, L 6 ¼", R4, V9 (Baumunk)

358 (L) Gasoline, **SUNSHINE IRON, MADE IN THE USA, PAT PENDING**, early 1900, L 7 ½", R1, V6
(M) Gasoline, **THE MONITOR, PAT APRIL 14 1903**, made by John Lake of Prairie Ohio, L 7", R1, V5
(R) Gasoline, **IMPERIAL BRASS MFG CO, CHICAGO ILL, MODEL 15 SELF HEATING IRON, PATENTED**, early 1900, L 6 ½", R1, V5

359 (L) Gasoline, **THE IMPROVED EASY IRON, FOOTE MFG CO, DAYTON O**, early 1900, L 7", R3, V6
(M) Gasoline, **SUN MFG CO, SOUTH BEND IND, USA, THE IRON THAT SIZZLES, PAT OCT 19 '04**, L 7", R3, V7
(R) Gasoline, early 1900, L 7 ¼", R1, V5

360 (L) Gasoline, **JUBILEE IRON, OMAHA NEB, PAT OCT 31 1899, JUNE 7 1904**, pat. by William Pitt of Independence, Mo, L 6 ⅝", R3, V8
(M) Gasoline, **HELP MATE, HERZ MFG CO, ST. PAUL, MINN., USA, PAT'D APLD FOR**, about 1900, L 7 ⅛", R2, V7
(R) Gasoline, **IMPERIAL SELF HEATING FLAT IRON**, The Imperial Brass Mfg Co, Chicago, Ill, pat. Feb 11 '11, L 6 ⅛", R1, V6

361 (L) Gasoline, **COMFORT IRON, SELF HEATING**, early 1900, L 7", R2, V6
(M) Gasoline, early 1900, L 7 1/4", R1, V6
(R) Gasoline, similar to **(L)**, early 1900, L 6 7/8", R1, V6

362 (L) Gasoline, **MARION SAD IRON CO, MARION COUNTY, PAT 1889**, rectangular top, sole removable, L 5 3/4", R4, V9 (Borsch)
(M) Natural Gas, **IWANTU COMFORT GAS IRON #6, STRAUSE GAS IRON CO, PHILA PA, PAT 1910**, L 6", R1, V5
(R) Gasoline, about 1930, L 7 3/4", R2, V4

363 (L) Gasoline, **DIAMOND, THE AKRON LAMP CO, AKRON OHIO, SELF HEATING IRON**, early 1900, L 7 3/8", R1, V5
(M) Gasoline, Argentina, **ROLIER, ARGENTINA**, all brass, early 1900, L 7 3/8", R4, V8
(R) Gasoline, **PAT APPLIED FOR 135-5988**, early 1900, L 8", R2, V7

364 (L) Gasoline, **THE DIAMOND IRON, MFG BY THE AKRON LAMP CO, AKRON OHIO, PAT APPD FOR, MADE IN USA**, early 1900, L 7 1/2", R1, V5
(M) Gasoline, **THE COLEMAN, COLEMAN LAMP CO, PHILA, CHICAGO, LOS ANGELES**, about 1925, L 7 3/8", R1, V4
(R) Gasoline, **MODEL 52059870**, early 1900, L 6 7/8", R2, V6

365 (L) Gasoline, **WARDS QUICK LIGHTING GASOLINE IRON, MONTGOMERY WARD, USE ONLY APPROVED GASOLINE** and more, pump in handle, about 1930, L 7 1/4", R1, V4
(M) Gasoline, **AMERICAN, AMERICAN GAS & MACHINE CO INC, ALBERT LEA, MINNESOTA**, black enamel surface, pump in handle, about 1930, L 7 1/2", R3, V7
(R) Gasoline, valve at back, early 1900, L 7 1/2", R4, V8

366 (L) Gas Jet, **W.F. SHAW'S PATENT SEPT 1 1857**, holes in top surface to allow burned gases from gas jet to flow-through body, L 6 1/4", R4, V8
(M) Gas Jet, **LFB**, hollow body flow-through style, early 1900, L 6", R4, V8
(R) Gas Jet, English, **R & A MAIN LTD GAS IRON, No. 400**, hollow body flow-through style, early 1900, L 5 1/2", R4, V9 (Carson)

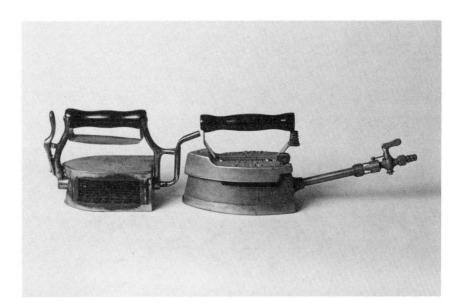

367 (L) Natural Gas, English, **J.W. WRIGHT CO, BIRMINGHAM**, with chimney and copper heat shield, about 1900, L 6", R3, V8 (Balestri)
(M) Natural Gas, revolving, late 1800, L 6", R5, V10 (Balestri)
(R) Natural Gas, English, **THE DAVIS "CRYSTAL" LUTON**, early 1900, L 5 3/4", R3, V8 (Balestri)

368 (L) Natural Gas, revolving, Trent, front latch and heat shield, early 1900, L 5 3/8", R5, V10 (Walker)
(R) Natural Gas, **NU-STYL PAT PEND, LA RUE GAS IRON, PAT APD FOR, 8 LBS**, 2 lb top cover can be removed changing iron from 8 lb to 6 lb, early 1900, L 7", R5, V11 (Walker)

369 (L) Natural Gas, revolving, **CROCKER AND FARNSWORTH, PAT MAR 20 '77**, latch in front, L 5 ⁵/₈", R5, V10 (Holtzman)
(R) Natural Gas, English, turned chimney **BEETALL, THE BEETALL MFG CO, BIRMINGHAM, ENGLAND** engraved on brass medallion, late 1800, L 6 ¼", R4, V9 (Holtzman)

370 (L) Natural Gas, English, **SALTERS GAS IRON**, mfg'd by Salter & Co. Ltd, West Bromwich, England, early 1900, L 6 ¼", R3, V9 (Baumunk)
(M) Natural Gas, English, **HOT CROSS, BRITISH MADE, 1 PATENT No .440820**, mfg'd by Wm. Cross & Son Ltd, West Bromwich, England, early 1900, L 5 ½", R3, V9 (Baumunk)
(R) Natural Gas, English, **OTTO, PAT No. 226721/24, IMPROVED PATENT**, mfg'd by William Cross & Son Ltd, West Bromwich, England, early 1900, L 7", R3, V9 (Baumunk)

371 (L) Natural Gas, English, **CLARKS FAIRY PRINCE No. 374, C B REG No. 781179**, blue enamel, plastic handle, mid 1900, L 6 ½", R4, V8
(R) Natural Gas, **THE FLETCHR LAUREL**, gray/white speckled agate, early 1900, L 6 ³/₈", R4, V9

372 (L) Natural Gas, **THE UNEEDIT GAS IRON, MFG BY THE ROSENBAUM MFG CO, NEW YORK, PAT PENDING**, early 1900, L 6 ½", R2, V7
(R) Natural Gas, heat shield with asbestos, early 1900, L 6 ½", R3, V7

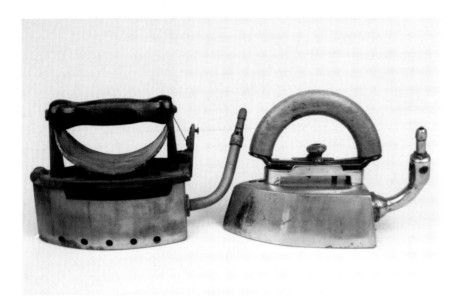

373 (L) Natural Gas, **BLESS & DRAKE, NEWARK NJ, PAT APP FOR**, hinged in front, early 1900, L 6 1/4", R3, V8 (Holtzman)
(R) Natural Gas, removable wood handle with thumbscrew to hold handle tight, early 1900, L 6 1/4", R4, V9 (Holtzman)

374 (L) Natural Gas, with chimney, early 1900, L 6 1/4", R3, V7
(R) Natural Gas, **DIAMOND HARDWARE MFG CO, PITTSBURGH PA**, with chimney and burn protector, early 1900, L 6 3/8", R4, V8

375 (L) Natural Gas, **JOHNSON IRON, RACINE WIS, PAT APP FOR**, early 1900, L 6 1/4", R3, V7
(R) Natural Gas, **THE PERFECT GAS IRON, BLESS & DRAKE, NEWARK NJ, PATD APR 8 1913**, L 6 1/4", R3, V7

376 (L) Natural Gas, early 1900, L 7", R1, V6
(M) Natural Gas, early 1900, L 6 3/8", R1, V6
(R) Natural Gas, **HERMIT, PAT AUG 22 1911**, L 6 3/4", R3, V7

116

377 (L) Natural Gas, **THE SWING, PAT DEC 4 1900**, black enamel surface, L 6 $^1/_2$", R3, V7
(R) Natural Gas, **THE SWING, PAT FEB 23 1904**, L 6 $^5/_8$", R3, V7

378 (L) Natural Gas, early 1900, L 6 $^5/_8$", R2, V7
(M) Natural Gas, **ACETYLENE STOVE MFG CO, CLEVELAND OHIO, PAT APPLD FOR**, early 1900, L 6", R2, V6
(R) Natural Gas, **NEW YORK PRESSING IRON CO**, hinged top, early 1900, L 6 $^3/_8$", R3, V7

379 (L) Natural Gas, **UNEEDIT GAS IRON, MADE BY THE ROSENBAUM MFG CO, NEW YORK, PATENTED AUG 19, SEPT 23 1913**, L 6 $^1/_2$", R1, V6
(M) Natural Gas, **HUMPHREY, GENERAL SPECIALITY CO, NY, PAT No. 106 2350** and others, early 1900, L 7 $^1/_4$", R3, V7
(R) Natural Gas, **IWANTU COMFORT, DOUBLE POINT, STRAUSE GAS IRON CO, PHILA PA**, early 1900, L 7 $^1/_2$", R1, V6

380 (L) Natural Gas, **WRIGHT, PAT AUG 22 1911**, L 7", R1, V6
(M) Natural Gas, **PAT APP'D FOR**, early 1900, L 6 $^1/_2$", R1, V6
(R) Natural Gas, **VULCAN GAS IRON 764, WM CRANE CO, NY, PAT APPLD FOR**, early 1900, L 6 $^1/_4$", R1, V6

381 (L) Natural Gas, **GME, PAT AUG 13 1901, OTHER PATS PENDG**, L 6", R3, V6
(M) Natural Gas, **GROSSBAR, PAT'D MARCH 9 1915**, L 6 1/8", R3, V7
(R) Natural Gas, **CENTRAL FLAT IRON MFG CO, BINGHAMPTON NY, PAT APR 23 '07, OTHER PATS PENDING**, L 6 3/8", R3, V6

382 (L) Natural Gas, **CENTRAL FLAT IRON MFG CO, BINGHAMPTON NY, PAT APR 23 '07, OPEN BLOW THRU IRON FROM FRONT - LIGHT - CLOSE**, L 6 1/4", R3, V7
(M) Natural Gas, **CENTRAL MFG CO, BINGHAMPTON NY, PAT APR 23 1907, MODEL K, TRADE IME MARK**, L 6 1/2", R3, V7
(R) Natural Gas, like **(M)**, **MODEL M, 5 LBS**, L 6 1/2", R3, V7

383 (L) Natural Gas, **SCHREIBER & GOLDBERG, NY**, early 1900, L 6", R3, V7
(R) Natural Gas, like **(L)**, L 5 3/4", R3, V7

384 (L) Natural Gas, **THE GLOBE GAS IRON CO, BOSTON MASS, PATENTED MARCH 11 1890**, L 10 1/2", R3, V7
(M) Natural Gas, **WM CRANE & CO, NY**, late 1800, L 10 1/8", R3, V7
(R) Natural Gas, late 1800, L 11", R2, V6

TAILOR AND COMMERCIAL IRONS

All those large and cumbersome irons that normally would not be found in a home are considered tailor and commercial irons. Tailor irons were manufactured in all the major categories of irons already presented in this book - i.e., charcoal, slug, liquid fuel and flat irons. In some cases, a true tailor iron was placed in another category such as charcoal or liquid fuel in order to show variation in models and to make it easily found by the reader.

Collector Hints

An abundance of commercial tailor irons are still available and prices are very reasonable. These irons have never been collected heavily because they are massive and difficult to display. Some models, however, are very rare. Collecting various sizes from specific foundries/manufacturers is a good approach. Always look for those with decorations, brass handles or unusual shapes. No reproductions are know.

385 (L) Cold Handle, **BENNS IXL No. 24**, open twisted handle, about 1900, L 10", R3, V7 (Balestri)
(R) Cast, **J.L. HAVEN & CO, 3, PAT**, handle has two crows eating an ear of corn, late 1800, L 9 3/4", R5, V12 (Balestri)

386 (L) Cast, train iron with smoke as handle, late 1800, R5, V12 (Kelley)
(R) Cast, #4, pat. Sept 2, 1873 by Joseph Hargrove, Cinn., Ohio, handle has two crows eating an ear of corn, R5, V12 (Kelley)

387 (L) Cast, **WAPAK #12**, about 1900, L 9 ¹/₄", R3, V6 (Holtzman)
(R) Cold Handle, **T.R. TIMBY, POTTSTOWN PA, PAT NOV 18 1851**, handle lifts off,
L 10 ³/₄", R5, V11 (Holtzman)

388 (L-1) Wrought, handle forged with body, early 1800, L 11 ¹/₄", R3, V7
(L-2) Wrought, like **(L-1)**, L 9 ¹/₂", R3, V7
(L-3) Wrought, like **(L-1)**, L 9", R3, V7
(L-4) Wrought, handle applied to body, very thin body, mid 1800, L 9 ¹/₄", R4, V7

389 (L-1) Wrought, handle forged with body, early 1800, L 10 ¹/₂", R3, V7
(L-2) Wrought, like **(L-1)**, L 10 ¹/₄", R3, V7
(L-3) Wrought, like **(L-1)**, L 11 ¹/₄", R3, V7
(L-4) Wrought, like **(L-1)**, L 8 ¹/₄", R3, V7

390 (L-1) Cast, late 1800, L 9 ³/₄", R3, V6
(L-2) Cast, brass handle, late 1800, L 10", R4, V8
(L-3) Cast, **C** in **(shield)**, **18**, Colebrookdale, late 1800, L 9 ¹/₂", R2, V3
(L-4) Cast, the entire body curves, late 1800, L 10", R5, V9

391 (L) Cast, **OBER MFG CO, CHAGRIN FALLS O, #20**, late 1800, L 9 ³/₄", R4, V8
(M) Cast, **THE OBER MFG CO, CHAGRIN FALLS O, #12**, late 1800, L 8 ³/₄", R4, V8
(Carson)
(R) Cast, **OBER**, more not legible, late 1800, L 8 ¹/₈", R4, V8

392 (L) Cast, **XX, 20**, late 1800, L 11", R1, V3
(M) Cast, **C in (shield)**, **20**, from Colebrookdale, late 1800, L 10", R1, V3
(R) Cast, **KEEN & BRO, 10**, late 1800, L 8 ⁷/₈", R1, V3

393 (L-1) Cast, French, **7K**, late 1800, L 8 ³/₄", R3, V7
(L-2) Cast **SAVERY & CO, PHILADELPHIA, 14**, late 1800, L 8", R2, V6
(L-3) Cast, French, **3-K**, late 1800, L 7 ¹/₄", R3, V7 (Carson)
(L-4) Cast, French, **1**, late 1800, L 7 ¹/₂", R3, V7 (Carson)

394 (L) Cold Handle, **SENSIBLE, NRS & CO, GROTON NY, PAT SEPT 6 '87, 16**,
removable handle, L 9 ¹/₂", R4, V9 (Carson)
(M) Cold Handle, **SENSIBLE, NRS & CO, 16**, removable handle, late 1800, L 8 ¹/₂", R4,
V9
(R) Cold Handle, **8**, removable handle, late 1800, L 8 ¹/₈", R3, V7

395 (L) Slug, Scandinavian, lift-up gate, about 1900, L 8", R3, V7
(R) Slug, lift-up hatch for slug, late 1800, L 11 ¹/₄", R3, V8

396 (L) Charcoal, German, **DRGM**, rear hinged top, angled chimney, early 1900, L 9 ³/₈", R3, V7
(M) Charcoal, turned chimney with lift-off top, **(star)** on back damper, early 1900, L 9 ¹/₂", R3, V7
(R) Electric, **HOT POINT, EDISON ELECTRIC APPLIANCE CO**, rear rheostat control, early 1900, L 10 ¹/₂", R2, V4

397 (L) Natural Gas, **NEW YORK PRESSING IRON CO, PAT APPLD FOR, #16**, early 1900, L 8 ³/₈", R2, V7
(M) Natural Gas, **KOENIG GAS IRON MFG CO, PHILA PA, K-5-14**, early 1900, L 8", R2, V7
(R) Natural Gas, **ROSENBAUM MFG CO, MAKERS ROSE GAS IRONS, PAT JUN 12 1906, NOV 17 1908, NEW YORK NY**, L 9 ¹/₄", R2, V7

398 (L) Natural Gas, **J. GROSS, PAT'D NOV 3 '92, No. 10**, L 11", R2, V7
(M) Natural Gas, **THE STEWART IRON, CENTRAL MFG CO, BINGHAMPTON NY, PATENTED JAN 29 1901**, L 9 ⁷/₈", R3, V7
(R) Natural Gas, late 1800, L 7", R3, V7

399 (L-1) Alcohol, European, burner/tank missing, early 1900, L 9 ¹/₂", R2, V6
(L-2) Cast, **GENESEE VALLEY MFG CO, MT MORRIS NY, #20**, late 1800, L 8 ¹/₄", R3, V5
(L-3) Cast, **C**, late 1800, L 8", R1, V4
(L-4) Cast, European, **3**, early 1900, L 6 ³/₄", R3, V5

400 (L) Steam, **KOENIG, NEW JERSEY**, early 1900, L 11 ¹/₄", R2, V6
(M) Steam, front thumb valve for heat control, early 1900, L 14 ¹/₂", R2, V6
(R) Steam, front thumb valve, early 1900, L 8 ¹/₄", R2, V6

401 (L-1) Steam, **N. RUBENSTEIN'S STEAM IRON, PAT 1327766, NY**, thumb valve, early 1900, L 10 ¹/₄", R2, V6
(L-2) Steam, **KOENIG, 10**, thumb valve, early 1900, L 10 ¹/₄", R2, V6
(L-3) Steam, **KOENIG ALL STEAM IRON, PHILA PA, PAT OCT 3 1924**, thumb valve, L 11 ³/₄", R2, V6
(L-4) Steam, **KOENIG ALL STEAM IRON, PHILA PA, PAT OCT 3 1924**, thumb valve, L 11 ³/₄", R2, V6

402 (L) Steam, **SCHREIBER & GOLDBERG, NEW YORK NY, COMPLETE EQUIPMENT AND SUPPLIES FOR GARMENT TRADE**, early 1900, L 6 ¹/₄", R2, V6
(R) Steam, **STEAM PRESSING IRON, PATRICK, DULUTH, PAT MAY 8 1906 AND OTHERS, CHICAGO, ILLINOIS**, L 6", R2, V6

ELECTRIC IRONS

Dating back to the turn of the century, the use of electricity revolutionized the method of heating irons. For the first time, the danger associated with burning coal, wood, or petroleum fluids was eliminated. Ingenious inventions followed which, over the years, added sophisticated electric improvements and gadgetry to the heating control and special function of the electric iron. Berney gives an account of how the electric iron was developed and how it has evolved. Future books on irons may focus solely on the electric iron due to the multitude of styles and availability of good material. This book has tried to show unusual examples of electric irons, but many more examples are available.

Collector Hints

Examples of electric irons can readily be found in excellent to mint-in-the-box condition at very reasonable if not cheap prices. I would urge that electric irons be collected now before prices increase. Availability of electric irons should not be a problem for many years due to the quantity that were mass produced.

403 (F) Double Pointed, Canadian, **C.W. BONGARD, TORONTO, No. 6D**, early 1900, L 7 1/4", R3, V7 (Fingerman)
(RL) White Enamel, **QUALITY IRON, IT'S WHITE & RIGHT, QUALITY APPLIANCE CO, RIVERSIDE ILL, USA, PAT 2/26/24**, L 7 3/8", R3, V7 (Fingerman)
(RR) White Enamel, **GENERAL ELECTRIC, PAT #1,612,114**, mid 1900, L 7 1/2", R2, V6 (Fingerman)

404 (F) Agate, English, **BRITISH DIAMIY, VOLTAGE 230**, early 1900, L 6 1/2", R3, V8 (Holtzman)
(M) CROWN MFG CO, ST LOUIS MO, fat body, early 1900, L 7", R3, V7 (Holtzman)
(R) HOT POINT, early 1900, L 6", R3, V6 (Holtzman)

405 (L) PETIPOINT, MODEL No. 410, WAVERLY TOOL CO, SANDUSKY OHIO, Art Deco style, about 1940, L 10", R4, V9 (Sinclair)
(F) Round, European, **BELGIUM**, small pointed toe, about 1950, Dia 5 $^1/_8$", R4, V9 (Baumunk)
(B) Round, **ROUND IRON, MODEL K, ROUND IRON CO, DETROIT USA**, about 1940, Dia 8", R4, V9 (Baumunk)
(R) Pyrex, **DETROIT APPLIANCE INC**, white inside, about 1940, L 7 $^1/_2$", R4, V12(Sinclair)

406 (L) Curtain Steamer, about 1925, R4, V8 (Kelley)
(R) French, **GABRIFER**, self contained trivet, about 1940, R3, V7 (Kelley)

407 (L) Travel, English, **PRILECT TRAVELING IRON**, orig tin box, about 1925, L 4 $^7/_8$", R3, V6 (Carson)
(M) Round, **K & M, FLAT WORK IRONER, KNAPP MONARCH CO, ST LOUIS**, about 1935, Dia 5 $^7/_8$", R3, V8
(R) Travel, English, **SMOOTHIE, LUCAS HOLDER LTD, COVENTRY**, orig box, about 1950, L 3 $^3/_8$", R3, V6

408 (L-1) THE ELECTRICAL & MFG CO, ST LOUIS MO, early 1900, L 5 $^3/_8$", R3, V6 (Holtzman)
(L-2) THE PROMETHING ELECTRICAL CO, PATENTED JAN 10 '99, AP 7 '08, L 5 $^1/_2$", R3, V6 (Holtzman)
(L-3) SEM, with stand in handle when flipped over, early 1900, L 5 $^1/_2$", R4, V8 (Holtzman)
(L-4) Steam, Australian, **TWYLITE SUPER STEAM IRON, APPROVALS BOARD, 240 V, 600 W, CAT #54**, early 1900, L 7", R4, V8 (Holtzman)

409 (FL) Steam, **WM CISSEL MFG CO, LOUISVILLE KY**, various steam ports around base, about 1940, L 7", R2, V4
(FR) PROCTOR SPEED IRON, PROCTOR & SCHWARTZ ELECTRIC CO, PHILA PA, about 1940, L 7", R2, V3
(RL) HANDY HOT, STREAMLINE, CHICAGO ELECTRIC MFG CO, heat indicator, about 1925, L 7 1/2", R2, V4
(RR) FOSTORIA, W BERSTED MFG CO, heat indicator, about 1925, L 7 1/2", R2, V4

410 (FL) Cordless, **EUREKA, CORDLESS AUTOMATIC, EUREKA, WILLIAMS CORP, DETROIT**, shoe is electric outlet, about 1950, L 7 1/2", R3, V5
(FR) Travel, **FEATHERLINE CORP, NEW YORK**, about 1950, L 7 3/4", R2, V3
(RL) AMERICAN BEAUTY, AM. ELECT. HEATER CO, DETROIT, clear red handle grip, heat indicator, about 1950, L 7 3/4", R2, V3
(RR) Like **(RL)**, amber grip, L 7 3/4", R2, V3

411 (L) Steam, **STEAM ELECTRIC CORP**, aluminum surface, about 1925, L 9 1/8", R2, V3
(M) Steam, **SILEX, THE SILEX CO, HARTFORD, CONN**, about 1925, L 9 1/4", R2, V3
(R) Fat Body, **CROWN MFG CO, ST LOUIS MO**, early 1900, L 7 3/8", R3, V7 (Carson)

412 (FL) AIR FLOW, CHIEF ELECTRICS INC, WINSTED CONN, heat indicator, about 1930, L 7 7/8", R2, V3
(FR) WESTINGHOUSE, about 1950, L 7 3/4", R1, V2
(RL) ALURON, THE WARING CORP, NY, white porcelain, orig box, about 1940, L 7 1/4", R2, V5
(RR) GENERAL ELECTRIC AUTOMATIC IRON, orig box, about 1950, L 7 1/2", R1, V2

126

413 (FL) GENERAL ELECTRIC, about 1960, L 6 ⁵/₈", R1, V2
(FR) PROCTOR, NEVER LIFT DELUX, button in handle releases the self contained stand, about 1950, L 7", R3, V5
(RL) HOT POINT, HEAT-O-MATIC, orig box, about 1925, L 6 ⁷/₈", R2, V3
(RR) SUNBEAM, orig tin box, about 1920, L 5 ³/₈", R3, V4

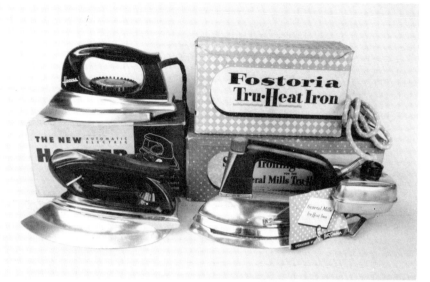

414 (FL) UNIVERSAL STROKE SAV-R, orig tag, about 1950, L 9", R1, V2
(FR) GENERAL MILLS, FOSTORIA TRU-HEAT IRON, with steam base shoe and water tank, all orig tags and 2 boxes, about 1950, L 9 ³/₄", R3, V6
(RL) THE NEW HOOVER IRON, HOOVER CO, NORTH CANTON OHIO, orig box, after 1950, L 7 ¹/₂", R1, V2
(RR) Boxes for **(FR)**

415 (FL) Iron with Curling Iron Heater, **UNIVERSAL, LANDERS, FRARY, CLARK, NEW BRITAIN CONN**, about 1930, L 5 ³/₄", R3, V4
(FR) Travel, Japan, all china, about 1930, L 5 ¹/₈", R4, V6
(RL) Early, French, **GALOR**, late 1800, L 6 ¹/₂", R2, V3
(RR) Early, European, late 1800, L 6 ¹/₄", R2, V3

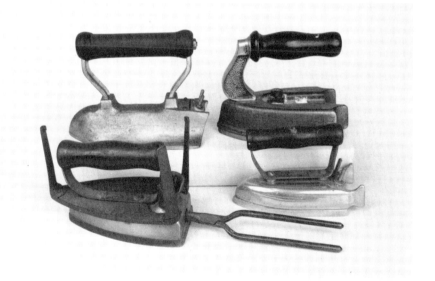

416 (FL) HOTPOINT, PACIFIC ELECTRIC HEATING CO, holds curling iron, reverse stand on handle, about 1915, L 5 ¹/₂", R3, V4
(FR) Travel, **WAAGE TRAVELER'S IRON, WAAGE ELECTRIC CO, CHICAGO**, stand at back, about 1925, L 5 ³/₈", R3, V4
(RL) Early, about 1900, L 6 ⁷/₈", R2, V3
(RR) PELOUZE, pat. 1912, Chicago, L 6", R3, V7

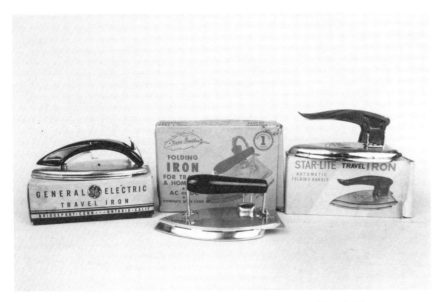

417 **(L)** Travel, **GENERAL ELECTRIC**, orig box, about 1950, L 6 ¼", R2, V4
(M) Travel, **FOLDING IRON, FIERY FEATHER, GEORGE MFG CO, YOUNGSTOWN OHIO**, orig box, about 1950, L 6 ¾", R2, V4
(R) Travel, Japan, **STAR-LITE**, orig box, about 1960, L 7", R1, V3

418 **(FL)** Travel, English, **PRILECT UNIVERSAL**, changeable voltage, after 1960, L 5 ¾", R3, V5 (Carson)
(FM) Travel, **KM KNAPP MONARCH**, about 1940, L 6 ⅜", R2, V4
(FR) Travel, **KM GAD-A-BOUT**, heat indicator, about 1950, L 7 ¾", R2, V4   with cord
(RL) Travel, **UNIVERSAL**, about 1950, L 7", R2, V3
(RM) Travel, Japan, **WTC**, about 1930, L 6", R2, V3
(RR) Travel, **ATC**, about 1950, L 6 ¾", R2, V3

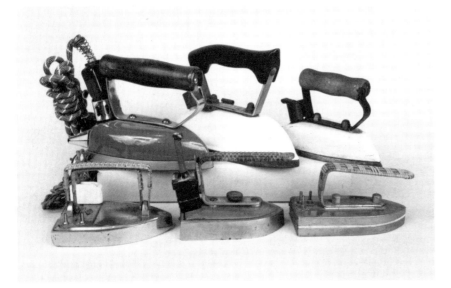

419 **(FL)** Travel, European, **SIET**, early 1900, L 5", R2, V4
(FM) Travel, European, **WARMAG**, early 1900, L 5", R2, V4
(FR) Travel, European, **ELHIEKO**, early 1900, L 5 ⅜", R2, V4
(RL) DOMINO ARISTOCRAT, DOMINION ELECTRICAL MFG CO, MINNEAPOLIS, MINN, green porcelain, about 1925, L 6 ½", R3, V7 (Carson)
(RM) European, **GRAETZOR**, white porcelain, about 1925, L 7 ¾", R3, V6 (Carson)
(RR) Yellow Porcelain, about 1925, L 5 ⅝", R2, V5

420 **(L)** Tie Press, pat. Oct 27, 1931, by David Benford, NYC, aluminum and fiber construction, L 19 ½", R1, V3
(R) Seam Press, **EMPIRE ELECTRICAL CO, CINCINNATI OHIO, PATENT PEND**, pat. on Nov 29, 1932, by Roland Bollman, L 10 ⅜", R1, V3

SMALL IRONS

Irons that are about 5" or smaller are considered small irons. Many of these irons were not made solely for children, but others were made as toys. Some small-sized irons have been pictured in this book with their larger sized counterparts in order to show the size difference which is difficult to convey when irons are shown in separate pictures in different parts of the book. An example of this is the cold handle, flat iron, Weida.

The small iron section includes all heating types that were previously discussed - i.e., charcoal, slug, fluters, goffering, special purpose and liquid fuel. Two books by Judy Politzer provide more information on small irons, including exact tracings of the base configurations of all her pictured irons[5,6]

.Collector Hints

Small irons are wonderful subjects to collect. Hundreds of examples were manufactured and availability at reasonable prices is still not a problem. These irons are quite desirable and they can be easily and tastefully displayed. As with the regular sized irons, look for the more decorative and those with makers' names and patent dates. Original paint enhances the desirability and value especially for the cast swans which were produced in blue, red and yellow paint with pin striping. Reproduction of small irons is a major problem that will likely accelerate as prices of the rare originals increase. To aid in detecting a reproduction, look for coarse grinding/sanding marks on the bottom and edges as well as poor patina. Rusting and pitting may be a means to hide newness. In the European brass reproductions, look for the wear that each iron should have received over 50 - 100 years of handling.

Known reproductions occur in the various categories of small irons - swans, cross rib, cylinder grip, rope grip, crosshatch, wire handle, Dutch brass, English brass and others. Be careful and if buying from a dealer, ask for a guarantee that each iron is old.

421 (L-1) Slug, Scottish, brass posts and finials, with companion brass trivet, top lifts off for slug, mid 1800, L 4", R5, V12 (Walker)
(L-2) Slug, like (L-1), L 3 3/8", R5, V12 (Walker)
(L-3) Slug, like (L-1), spring latch, L 3 7/8", R5, V12 (Walker)
(L-4) Slug, like (L-1), L 3 3/4", R5, V12 (Walker)

422 (L) Drop-In-The-Back, slug, Dutch, brass with companion trivet, late 1800, L 2", R5, V10 (Kelley)
(M) Drop-In-The-Back, like (L), L 3", R5, V10 (Kelley)
(R) Drop-In-The-Back, like (L), L 4", R5, V10 (Kelley)

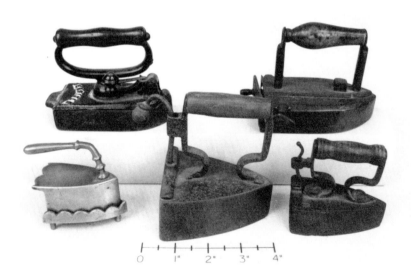

423 (FL) Drop-In-The-Back, slug, Dutch, brass with companion trivet, late 1800, L 2 1/8", R5, V10
(FM) Slug, English, late 1800, L 3 3/8", R4, V9
(FR) Slug, English, pieced construction, mid 1800, L 2 7/8", R5, V10
(RL) Slug, SENSIBLE, NRS & CO, GROTON NY, late 1800, L 3 3/4", R5, V10
(RR) Slug, European, brass, mid 1800, L 4 1/8", R5, V9 (Carson)

424 (L-1) Slug, English, #2, all brass, lift-up gate, late 1800, L 3 7/8", R3, V8
(L-2) Slug, like (L-1) hinged gate, late 1800, L 3 1/4", R4, V8
(L-3) Slug, like (L-1), lift-up gate, late 1800, L 2 7/8", R4, V8
(L-4) Slug, like (L-1), L 2 3/4", R4, V9
(L-5) Slug, like (L-1), L 1 7/8", R5, V10

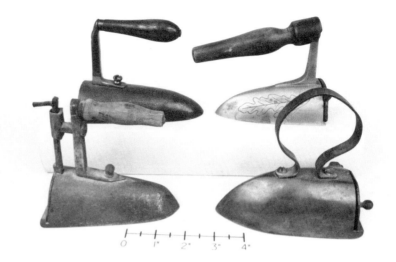

425 (L) Ox Tongue, slug, European, all brass with companion trivet, mid 1800, L 4 $^7/_8$", R4, V9
(M) Ox Tongue, slug, like **(L)**, L 4 $^1/_8$", R4, V9
(R) Ox Tongue, slug, like **(L)**, leather wrapped handle, L 4 $^1/_8$", R4, V9

426 (FL) Ox Tongue, slug, mid 1800, L 4 $^5/_8$", R4, V9
(FR) Ox Tongue, slug, brass, late 1800, L 5", R3, V8
(RL) Ox Tongue, slug, early 1800, L 5 $^1/_8$", R4, V9
(RR) Ox Tongue, slug, brass engraved, late 1800, L 4 $^1/_4$", R4, V9 (Carson)

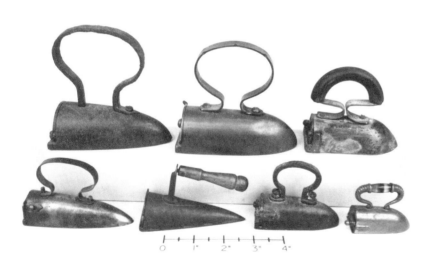

427 (FL-1) Slug, European, about 1900, L 3 $^3/_4$", R3, V7
(FL-2) Slug, like **(FL-1)**, mid 1800, L 3 $^5/_8$", R5, V9
(FL-3) Slug, like **(FL-1)**, all brass, late 1800, L 2 $^7/_8$", R4, V9
(FL-4) Tape Measure, English, brass, late 1800, L 2 $^1/_8$", R3, V9
(RL) Slug, European, late 1800, L 4 $^1/_4$", R3, V8
(RM) Slug, European, about 1900, L 4 $^1/_4$", R2, V7
(RR) Slug, European, about 1900, L 3 $^1/_2$", R3, V7

428 (L-1) Rocker Fluter, **GENEVA FLUTER, PAT'D 1866**, L 3$^1/_2$", R5, V11
(L-2) Rocker Fluter, late 1800, L 1 $^7/_8$", R4, V9
(L-3) Rocker Fluter, late 1800, L 1 $^7/_{16}$", R5, V10
(L-4) Rocker Fluter, reproduction marked **DAVE IRONS 1991**, limited edition, all brass, L 1 $^7/_8$", R1, V4

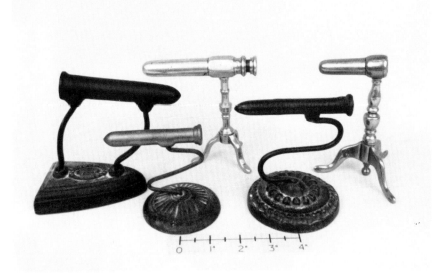

429 (FL) Goffer, English, about 1900, brass barrel, B 3 3/8", R3, V8
(FR) Goffer, like **(FL)**, iron barrel, B 3 7/8", R3, V7
(RL) Combination, **BULOCK CO**, handle is goffer, about 1900, L 3 7/8", R5, V12 (J. Irons)
(RM) Goffer, English, Queen Anne, brass, with screw-in plug, late 1800, B 4", R5, V10
(RR) Goffer, English, Queen Anne, brass, late 1800, B 2 3/8", R4, V9

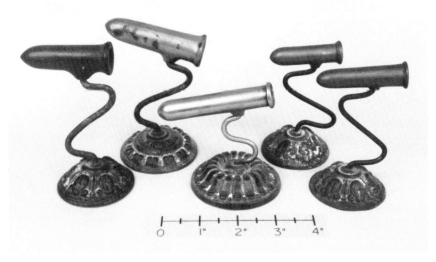

430 (FL) Goffer, English, **KENRICK**, about 1900, B 2 3/8", R3, V7
(FM) Goffer, English, brass barrel, about 1900, B 3 1/4", R3, V8
(FR) Goffer, like **(FL)**, brass barrel, B 2 1/4", R3, V7
(RL) Goffer, like **(FR)**, B 2 7/8", R3, V8
(RR) Goffer, like **(FR)** B 2", R3, V8

431 (L) Charcoal, European, jockey head on latch, late 1800, L 5 1/4", R3, V9
(M) Charcoal, European, bird head on latch, late 1800, L 4 3/8", R4, V9
(R) Charcoal, European, woman's head on latch, leather handle, late 1800, L 5", R3, V9
(J. Irons)

432 (L-1) Tall Chimney Charcoal, European, **H**, late 1800, L 3 1/2", R4, V9
(L-2) Charcoal, European, early 1900, L 4 1/4", R3, V8
(L-3) Charcoal, European, late 1800, L 4 1/8", R4, V9
(L-4) Toy Charcoal, German, green body, red handle, thin sheet metal, early 1900, L 2 3/4", R3, V6
(L-5) Toy Charcoal, European, thin metal, early 1900, L 2 1/8", R1, V4

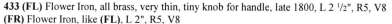

433 (FL) Flower Iron, all brass, very thin, tiny knob for handle, late 1800, L 2 ¹/₂", R5, V8
(FR) Flower Iron, like **(FL)**, L 2", R5, V8
(RL) Pan Iron, **CHINA**, thin brass with zinc plating, early 1900, Dia 3 ¹/₂", R2, V6
(RM) Pan Iron, **INDIA, 1953**, brass, Dia 2 ¹/₄", R1, V4
(RR) Pan Iron, **CHINA**, brass with plating, about 1930, Dia 1¹/₈", R3, V6

434 (L) Alcohol, **W.H. HOWELL CO, GENEVA ILL, PAT 11-14-11**, to heat turn iron upside down and fill small trough with fuel, burn all the fuel before using, L 3 ¹/₂", R4, V9 (Sinclair)
(R) All Cast, horse, European, late 1800, L 3 ¹/₂", R5, V12 (Sinclair)

435 (L-1) Wrought, sawtooth edge decoration, mid 1800, L 4 ³/₄", R3, V6
(L-2) Wrought, edge decoration, mid 1800, L 3 ⁷/₈", R3, V7
(L-3) Wrought, **1792**, rare date, L 3 ³/₄", R5, V8
(L-4) Wrought, **1820**, rare date, L 3 ¹/₄", R5, V8

436 (L-1) Wrought, mid 1800, L 3 ¹/₂", R3, V7
(L-2) Wrought, late 1800, L 4", R3, V6
(L-3) Wrought, mid 1800, L 3 ³/₄", R3, V7
(L-4) Wrought, mid 1800, L 3 ³/₄", R3, V7
(L-5) Wrought, Mexican, early 1900, L 3", R2, V5

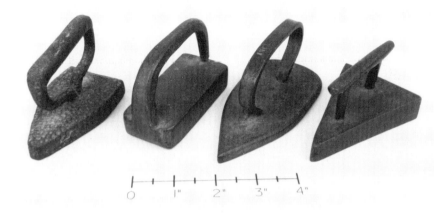

437 (L-1) Wrought, mid 1800, L 3$^{1}/_{8}$", R3, V6
(L-2) Wrought, mid 1800, L 3 $^{1}/_{4}$", R4, V8
(L-3) Wrought, mid 1800, L 4 $^{5}/_{8}$", R3, V6
(L-4) Wrought, mid 1800, L 3 $^{3}/_{8}$", R3, V7

438 (L) Cast, swan, by Ray M. Harpel, Sinking Springs, PA, early 1900, L 3 $^{3}/_{8}$", R5, V10 (Holtzman)
(R) Cast, swan, late 1800, L 4 $^{7}/_{8}$", R4, V9

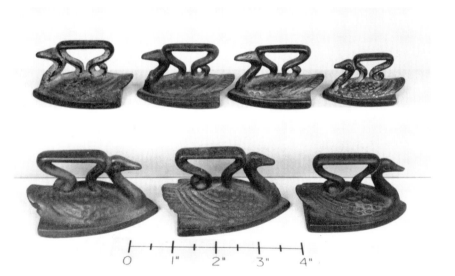

439 (FL) Cast, swan, old swans have mold break under beak, late 1800, L 2 $^{15}/_{16}$", R1, V6
(FM) Cast, swan, L 2 $^{3}/_{4}$", R1, V6
(FR) Cast, swan, L 2 $^{1}/_{2}$", R1, V6
(RL-1) Cast, swan, L 2 $^{1}/_{4}$", R1, V6
(RL-2) Cast, swan, L 2 $^{1}/_{8}$", R1, V6
(RL-3) Cast, swan, L 2 $^{1}/_{16}$", R1, V6
(RL-4) Cast, swan, L 1 $^{3}/_{4}$", R4, V9

440 (FL) Rope Handle, by Grey Iron Casting Co, right hand twist, early 1900, L 2 $^{3}/_{4}$", R5, V9 (Carson)
(FR) Cold Handle, **PET**, squeeze wire posts to remove handle, early 1900, L 3 $^{3}/_{4}$", R4, V9
(RL) Cast, swan, black painted surfce, late 1800, L 3 $^{1}/_{4}$", R5, V9 (Dreher)
(RR) Gas Jet, by Chalfant Mfg Co, pat. Jan 3, 1871, replaced handle, L 2 $^{7}/_{8}$", R4, V8

441 (L-1) Gas Jet, Chalfant Mfg Co, Jan 3, 1871, L 3", R4, V9 (Holtzman)
(L-2) Cold Handle, **OBER, PAT 1895, CHA. GALLS O**, removable handle, L 4", R4, V8 (Holtzman)
(L-3) Wood Handle, **CHALFANT MFG CO, PHILA, PAT JUNE 25 '78**, modified handle, L 3 ³/₈", R5, V8 (Holtzman)
(L-4) Strap Handle, European, all copper, late 1800, L 3 ³/₈", R5, V8 (Holtzman)
(L-5) Cast, English, painted red, early 1900, L 2 ¹/₂", R4, V8 (Holtzman)

442 (FL) Two Piece, about 1850, L 5 ¹/₈", R4, V8
(FR) Cast, **MRS. MARGARET YOUNG, B.I.E. DAY, NOV 8 1961**, L 4 ³/₈", R3, V7 (Carson)
(RL) Wrought, about 1850, L 5 ¹/₄", R4, V8
(RR) Two Piece, **M.L. TOVER**, slip-in handle, late 1800, L 3 ⁷/₈", R4, V8 (Carson)

443 (L) Cap, French, decorative casting, late 1800, L 5 ¹/₄", R5, V11 (Holtzman)
(M) Cap, French, decorative casting, late 1800, L 3 ¹/₄", R5, V11
(R) Cap, French, decorative casting, late 1800, L 2 ³/₄", R5, V11

444 (FL) Oval Cap, French, **WP**, late 1800, L 3 ⁷/₈", R2, V5
(FM) Oval Cap, like **(FL)**, **(wreath)**, L 3 ¹/₂", R2, V5
(FR) Oval Cap, English, **CARRON O**, late 1800, L 4", R2, V6
(RL) Oval Cap, like **(FL)**, **O**, L 3", R2, V5
(RM) Oval Cap, like **(FL)**, L 3 ¹/₂", R2, V5
(RR) Oval Cap, English, **KENRICK, #3**, late 1800, L 3 ⁷/₈", R2, V6

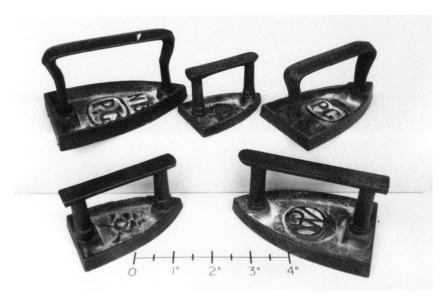

445 (FL) Cast, French, **(rose)**, late 1800, L 3", R3, V7
(FR) Cast, like **(FL)**, **WP**, L 3 ⁷/₈", R3, V6
(RL) Cast, like **(FL)**, **PG N3**, L 4", R1, V4
(RM) Cast, like **(FL)**, **(rose)**, L 2 ³/₈", R3, V7
(RR) Cast, like **(FL)**, **PG**, L 3 ¹/₂", R1, V4

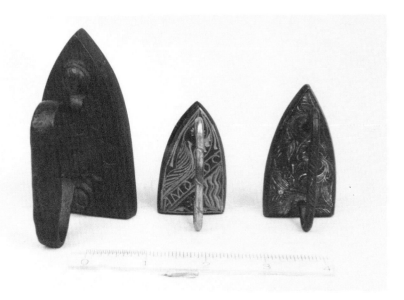

446 (L) Cast, French, **OR (flowers)**, late 1800, L 3 ³/₈", R4, V8 (Holtzman)
(M) Amozoc, Mexican, engraved designs, early 1900, L 2 ¹/₄", R4, V8 (Holtzman)
(R) Amozoc, Mexican, engraved designs, early 1900, L 2 ¹/₂", R4, V8

447 (L-1) Cast, French, **(face) GN**, late 1800, L 2 ³/₈", R4, V9 (Holtzman)
(L-2) Cast, like **(L-1)**, **(angel)**, L 3 ¹/₄", R4, V9
(L-3) Cast, like **(L-1)**, **(dog/bird in tree)**, L 3 ⁷/₈", R4, V9 (Holtzman)
(L-4) Cast, like **(L-1)**, **(boar)**, L 3 ⁷/₈", R4, V9 (Holtzman)
(L-5) Cast, like **(L-1)**, **(rooster)**, L 4", R4, V9 (Holtzman)

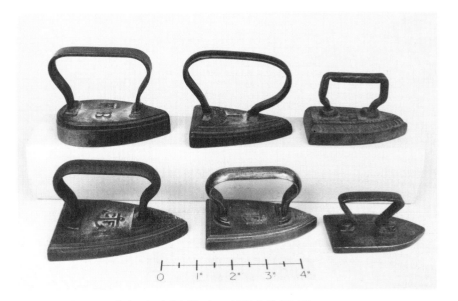

448 (FL) Cast, French, **(anchor) CF, #3**, about 1900, L 4", R2, V5
(FM) Cast, like **(FL)**, **#2**, L 3 ¹/₂", R2, V5 (Carson)
(FR) Cast, French, early 1900, L 3", R2, V4
(RL) Round Back, European, **FB**, about 1900, L 3 ⁵/₈", R3, V6
(RM) Cast, English, **GREEN #1**, late 1800, L 3 ¹/₄", R3, V6
(RR) Hollow Grip, Russian, late 1800, L 3 ¹/₄", R4, V8 (Carson)

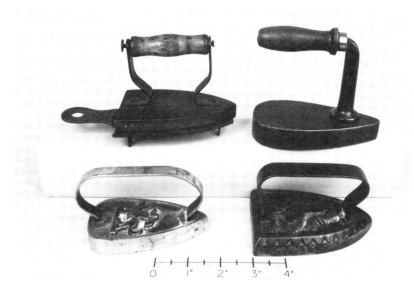

449 (L-1) Cast, French, teardrop, late 1800, L 3 ¼", R3, V7 (Holtzman)
(L-2) Wire Handle, French, **(star)**, teardrop, late 1800, L 4 ¼", R3, V6 (Holtzman)
(L-3) Wire Handle, French, thin base, early 1900, L 3 ⅜", R3, V6 (Holtzman)
(L-4) Wire Handle, Mexican, thin base, early 1900, L 3 ⅜", R2, V6 (Holtzman)

450 (FL) Cast, French, **(boy on lion)**, about 1900, L 3 ⅞", R4, V9 (Carson)
(FR) Cast, French, **(rooster)**, about 1900, L 4", R4, V9 (Carson)
(RL) Cast, French, late 1800, L 4", R3, V7 (Carson)
(RR) Round Back, European, late 1800, L 4 ⅜", R3, V7 (Carson)

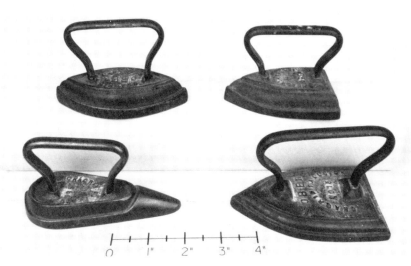

451 (FL) Cast, sleeve, **OBER, CHAGRIN FALLS O, #1**, about 1900, L 4 ½", R4, V9
(FR) Cast, **OBER, CHAGRIN FALLS O, No. 15**, about 1900, L 4 ⅜", R3, V8
(RL) Cast, **OBER, CHAGRIN FALLS O**, about 1900, L 4", R3, V8
(RR) Cast, **OBER, CHAGRIN FALLS O, #1**, about 1900, L 3 ⅜", R3, V8

452 (F) Cold Handle, **ENTERPRISE MFG CO, PHILA PA, JAN 1 '77, No. 115**, all iron, L 3 ⅞", R2, V6
(RL) Cold Handle, **ENTERPRISE MFG CO, PHILA, PAT IRON**, all iron, about 1900, open holes, L 2 ½", R3, V7
(RM) Cast, about 1900, L 2 ⅜", R2, V4
(RR) Cast, like **(RL)**, partial holes, L 2 ½", R2, V6

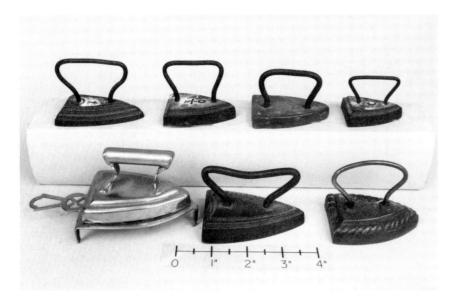

453 (FL) Hollow Grip, English, brass with trivet, late 1800, L 2 ⁷/₈", R4, V8
(FM) Wire Handle, about 1900, L 3", R3, V6
(FR) Wire Handle, Mexican, early 1900, L 2 ⁵/₈", R2, V5
(RL-1) Wire Handle, Mexican, early 1900, L 2 ⁵/₈", R1, V3
(RL-2) Wire Handle, (**key**), early 1900, L 2 ¹/₄", R1, V3
(RL-3) Wire Handle, lead base, early 1900, L 2 ¹/₂", R3, V4
(RL-4) Wire Handle, like **(RL-2)**, **O**, L 1 ³/₄", R2, V4

454 (FL) Wire Handle, about 1900, L 4", R3, V5
(FM) Wire Handle, about 1900, L 4 ³/₈", R3, V6
(FR) Wire Handle, European, 9 layers, about 1925, L 3 ¹/₂", R3, V7 (Carson)
(RL) Wire Handle, (**flower**), late 1800, L 4 ¹/₈", R3, V8 (Carson)
(RR) Wire Handle, about 1900, L 4 ¹/₈", R2, V5

455 (FL) Wire Handle, about 1900, L 3 ¹/₈", R2, V4
(FM) Wire Handle, (**4 stars**), about 1900, L 3 ³/₈", R3, V6
(FR) Wire Handle, Mexican, **#2**, early 1900, L 3 ¹/₄", R1, V3
(RL) Wire Handle, (**star**), about 1900, L 2 ⁷/₈", R3, V6
(RM) Wire Handle, English, **VRO**, late 1800, L 2 ¹/₄", R3, V6
(RR) Wire Handle, about 1900, L 3", R2, V5

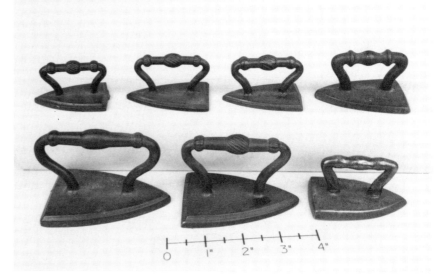

456 (FL) Tri-Bump, late 1800, L 3 ³/₈", R1, V4
(FM) Tri-Bump, like **(FL)**, L 3 ¹/₄", R1, V4
(FR) Tri-Bump, like **(FL)**, L 2 ¹/₄", R3, V6
(RL-1) Tri-Bump, like **(FL)**, L 2 ¹/₈", R1, V4
(RL-2) Tri-Bump, like **(FL)**, L 2 ³/₈", R1, V4
(RL-3) Tri-Bump, like **(FL)**, L 2 ³/₈", R1, V4
(RL-4) Tri-Bump, like **(FL)**, L 2 ¹/₂", R3, V6

457 (FL-1) Cylinder Grip, about 1900, L 3 ³/₄", R1, V4
(FL-2) Cylinder Grip, like **(FL-1)**, L 3 ³/₈", R1, V4
(FL-3) Cylinder Grip, like **(FL-1)** all brass, L 3 ¹/₄", R3, V5
(FL-4) Cylinder Grip, like **(FL-1)**, Colebrookdale Iron Co, about 1920, L 3 ³/₄", R3, V5
(RL-1) Rope, about 1900, L 2 ⁷/₈", R1, V3   **(RL-2)** Diamond Grip, early 1900, L 2 ⁷/₈", R1, V4
(RL-3) Cylinder Grip, like **(FL-1)**, L 3 ³/₈", R2, V4   **(RL-4)** Cylinder Grip, like **(FL-1)**, L 3 ¹/₈", R1, V4

458 (FL) Cylinder Grip, **O**, late 1800, L 3", R3, V7
(FM) Strap, brass base, late 1800, L 3 ¹/₈", R4, V8
(FR) Cylinder Grip, **(flower)**, late 1800, L 2 ⁷/₈", R3, V7
(RL) Cylinder Grip, **#3**, late 1800, L 2 ¹/₂", R3, V6
(RM) Strap, late 1800, L 2 ¹/₄", R3, V7 (Carson)
(RR) Cylinder Grip, late 1800, L 2 ¹/₈", R3, V6

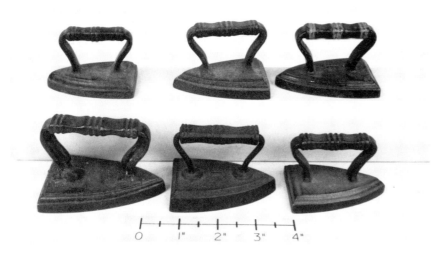

459 (FL) Cross Rib, by Grey Iron Casting Co, about 1900, L 3 ³/₈", R1, V4
(FM) Block Grip, J & E Stephens, #1, late 1800, L 2 ⁷/₈", R1, V4
(FR) Cross Rib, like **(FL)**, L 2 ³/₄", R1, V3
(RL) Cross Rib, like **(FL)**, L 2 ¹/₂", R1, V3
(RM) Cross Rib, like **(FL)**, L 2 ⁵/₈", R1, V3
(RR) Cross Rib, like **(FL)**, L 2 ⁷/₈", R1, V3

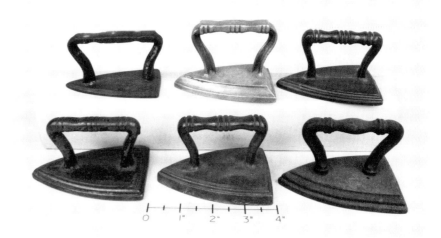

460 (FL) Cross Rib, English, late 1800, L 3 ³/₄", R3, V6
(FM) Cross Rib, like **(FL)**, L 3 ⁵/₈", R2, V5
(FR) Tri-Bump, late 1800, L 3 ⁷/₈", R2, V5
(RL) Cross Rib, like **(FL)**, L 3 ¹/₄", R2, V6
(RM) Cross Rib, brass, about 1900, L 3 ¹/₂", R3, V6
(RR) Cross Rib, like **(FL)**, L 3 ¹/₂", R3, V7

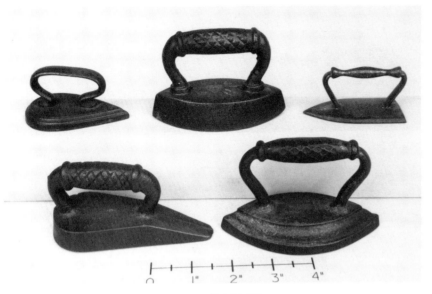

461(FL) Cross Hatch, sleeve, about 1900, L 4 $\frac{1}{8}$", R3, V7
(FR) Cross Hatch, late 1800, L 4 $\frac{1}{8}$", R3, V7
(RL) Round Back, European, about 1900, L 2 $\frac{7}{8}$", R3, V7
(RM) Cross Hatch, about 1900, L 3 $\frac{3}{4}$", R2, V5
(RR) Tri-Bump, English, about 1900, L 2 $\frac{3}{4}$", R2, V5

462 (FL) Rope, about 1900, L 4 $\frac{1}{2}$", R2, V5
(FM) Rope, about 1900, L 4 $\frac{1}{4}$", R1, V3
(FR) Rope, like **(FL)**, L 4 $\frac{1}{4}$", R2, V5
(RL) Rope, like **(FM)**, L 3 $\frac{3}{8}$", R1, V3
(RM) Rope, like **(FM)**, L 3", R1, V3
(RR) Rope, like **(FM)**, L 3 $\frac{5}{8}$", R1, V3

463 (FL) Block Grip, **BLACKLOCK #1**, about 1900, L 3 $\frac{1}{4}$", R4, V8 (Carson)
(FM) Block Grip, sleeve, **WALKER, BOSTON**, late 1800, L 4 $\frac{3}{4}$", R4, V7 (Carson)
(FR) Block Grip, **(keystone)**, late 1800, L 3 $\frac{3}{8}$", R3, V6
(RL) Block Grip, **DOWNS & CO #2**, late 1800, L 3 $\frac{7}{8}$", R3, V6
(RM) Block Grip, **GENEVA ILL, #2 $\frac{1}{2}$**, late 1800, L 4 $\frac{1}{4}$", R3, V6 (Carson)
(RR) Block Grip, Mexican, aluminum grip, about 1900, L 3 $\frac{5}{8}$", R3, V5 (Carson)

464 (FL) Block Grip, **WAPAK 2**, late 1800, L 4", R2, V6
(FM) Block Grip, **CHATTANOOGA IMPLT MFG CO**, late 1800, L 3 $\frac{1}{2}$", R4, V7
(FR) Block Grip, **D**, brass handle, late 1800, L 3 $\frac{1}{4}$", R4, V7
(RL-1) Block Grip, **ACW #1**, late 1800, L 3 $\frac{3}{8}$", R2, V6
(RL-2) Block Grip, **(cherries)**, about 1900, L 3 $\frac{1}{4}$", R3, V7
(RL-3) Block Grip, **ACW**, late 1800, L 2 $\frac{7}{8}$", R3, V6
(RL-4) Block Grip, **#2**, early 1900, L 2 $\frac{7}{8}$", R4, V7

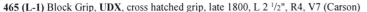

465 (L-1) Block Grip, **UDX**, cross hatched grip, late 1800, L 2 ¹/₂", R4, V7 (Carson)
(L-2) Block Grip, **(dog)**, same maker as **(L-1)**, L 1 ³/₄", R4, V8
(L-3) Block Grip, like **(L-2)**, L 2", R4, V8
(L-4) Block Grip, **(arrow)**, like **(L-2)**, L 1 ⁷/₈", R4, V8
(L-5) Block Grip, **(&)**, like **(L-2)**, L 1 ⁷/₈", R4, V8

466 (FL) Hollow Grip, English, **TOY #2**, late 1800, L 3 ³/₄", R4, V7 (Carson)
(FM) Hollow Grip, like **(FL)**, **#1**, L 3 ¹/₈", R4, V7 (Carson)
(FR) Hollow Grip, English, **KENRICK O**, late 1800, L 3", R3, V6
(RL-1) Hollow Grip, **#2**, late 1800, L 3", R3, V5
(RL-2) Hollow Grip, like **(RL-1)**, **#1**, L 2 ⁷/₈", R2, V4
(RL-3) Hollow Grip, like **(RL-1)**, 0, L 2 ⁷/₈", R2, V4
(RL-4) Hollow Grip, like **(RL-1)** L 2 ¹/₄", R3, V6

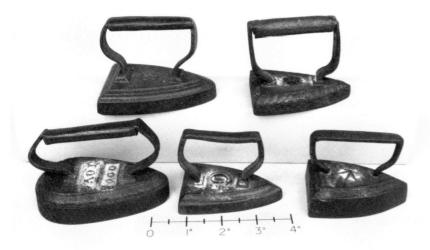

467 (FL) Hollow Grip, English, **DOG TOY**, late 1800, L 3 ³/₄", R4, V7
(FM) Hollow Grip, English, **O**, late 1800, L 3", R2, V5
(FR) Strap, **(star)**, late 1800, L 2 ⁷/₈", R3, V7 (Carson)
(RL) Hollow Grip, like **(FM)**, **#3**, L 3 ¹/₂", R2, V4
(RR) Hollow Grip, like **(FM)**, **(flower)**, L 3 ¹/₈", R3, V6

468 (L) Wood Grip, decorated top surface, possibly J & E Stevens Co of Conn, late 1800, L 3 ³/₄", R5, V8 (Holtzman)
(M) Wood Grip, decorated top surface, scalloped edge, possibly Stevens, L 3 ³/₈", R5, V8 (Holtzman)
(R) Wood Grip, **(5 pt star)**, Stevens, late 1800, L 3 ³/₈", R3, V7 (Holtzman)

469 (FL) Wood Grip, **THE GEM #2**, J & E Stevens Co, about 1900, L 4 ⁵/₈", R4, V8
(FR) Wood Grip, **25**, Stevens, about 1900, L 4 ¹/₂", R3, V8 (Carson)
(RL) Wood Grip, Mexican, about 1900, L 3 ¹/₈", R1, V4
(RR) Wood Grip, **THE GEM**, Stevens, about 1900, L 3 ⁷/₈", R3, V8 (Carson)

470 (FL) Wood Grip, **THE VICTOR #10**, by J & E Stevens Co of Conn, about 1900, L 3", R4, V8
(FM) Wood Grip, **(star)**, by Stevens, about 1900, L 3 ¹/₂", R3, V7
(FR) Wood Grip, like **(FM)**, L 2 ¹/₂", R4, V8
(RL) Wood Grip, **OUR PET**, by Stevens, L 3 ¹/₂", R3, V7 (Carson)
(RR) Wood Grip, like **(RL)**, L 2 ⁷/₈", R4, V8

471 (FL) Wood Grip, **THE PEARL**, late 1800, L 3 ³/₄", R3, V7
(FR) Wood Grip, **THE JEWEL SAD IRON**, Detroit Stove Works, about 1900, L 3 ⁷/₈", R4, V8
(RL) Wood Grip, **THE PEARL**, late 1800, L 2 ³/₄", R4, V8
(RM) Wood Grip, **(Liberty head)**, late 1800, L 3 ³/₄", R2, V6
(RR) Wood Grip, **(design)**, Grey Iron Casting Co, Mt Joy PA, about 1900, L 3", R3, V7

472 (FL) Make-Do, repaired handle, about 1900, L 3 ⁵/₈", R2, V4
(FM) Make-Do, repaired handle, about 1900, L 2 ³/₄", R2, V4
(FR) Make-Do, **THE PEARL**, repaired handle, about 1900, L 3 ⁷/₈", R2, V4
(RL) Wood Grip, **MADE IN USA**, about 1900, L 3 ¹/₄", R4, V6 (Carson)
(RM) Wood Grip, **DOVER USA**, about 1900, L 3 ¹/₂", R1, V4
(RR) Wood Grip, about 1900, L 3 ¹/₄", R2, V4 (Carson)

473 **(FL)** Two Piece, **SENSIBLE No. 0, NRS & CO**, about 1900, L 4", R2, V6
(FM) Two Piece, like **(FL)**, **No. 4**, L 5 ¹/₄", R2, V6
(FR) Two Piece, **PAT MAY 21 1893**, L 4 ³/₈", R3, V7
(RL) Two Piece, sleeve, about 1900, L 4 ³/₈", R3, V8
(RM) Two Piece, about 1900, L 3 ⁷/₈", R3, V7
(RR) Two Piece, like **(FL)**, L 3 ⁵/₈", R3, V7

474 **(FL)** Two Piece, **PAT APL 1895**, L 5", R3, V6
(FR) Two Piece, about 1900, L 3 ⁵/₈", R1, V5
(RL) Two Piece, about 1900, L 3 ¹/₂", R2, V6
(RM) Two Piece, about 1900, L 3 ¹/₄", R1, V4
(RR) Two Piece, about 1900, L 3 ³/₈", R1, V4

475 **(FL)** Two Piece, **ASBESTOS SAD IRON, PAT MAY 22 1900**, L 4", R1, V3
(FM) Two Piece, like **(FL)**, L 4 ³/₄", R1, V3
(FR) Two Piece, **DOVER SAD IRON No. 812**, early 1900, L 4", R1, V3
(RL-1) Two Piece, early 1900, L 3 ³/₈", R2, V4
(RL-2) One Piece, early 1900, L 3 ¹/₂", R2, V4
(RL-3) Two Piece, **DOVER SAD IRON No. 912**, early 1900, L 4 ¹/₈", R2, V3
(RL-4) Two Piece, early 1900, L 3 ³/₈", R3, V7

476 **(FL)** Two Piece, **DOVER SLEEVE IRON, MADE USA**, about 1900, L 5", R1, V4
(FR) Two Piece, **ASBESTOS SAD IRON, PAT MAY 22 1900**, L 4 ⁷/₈", R1, V4
(RL) Base for **(FR)**
(RR) Two Piece, **DOVER SAD IRON, #912**, early 1900, L 4 ⁵/₈", R1, V4

477 (FL) Cast, **(heart)**, late 1800, L 3 1/4", R5, V9
(FR) Cap, French, rough casting, late 1800, L 3 1/4", R5, V10
(RL) Give-Away, **DETMER WOOLEN CO, ONLY HOUSE WITH SEVEN
DISTRIBUTING STORES**, pin cushion top, about 1900, L 4", R4, V8
(RR) Two Piece, **ASBESTOS SAD IRON, SOUVENIR LEWIS & CLARK
EXPOSITION 1905**, L 3 7/8", R5, V9 (Eubanks)

478 (FL) Toy Electric, about 1930, L 3 3/4", R2, V3
(FR) Toy Mangle, **AN ARCADE TOY**, wood roller that turns, about 1930, Roll 3", R5, V9
(RL) Toy Electric, European, about 1925, L 3 7/8", R3, V6
(RR) Toy Slug, European, about 1925, L 3 5/8", R3, V5

479 (FL-1) Toy, about 1900, L 1 1/4", R2, V4
(FL-2) Toy, like **(FL-1)**, L 1 3/16", R2, V3   **(FL-3)** Toy, like **(FL-1)**, L 1 1/8", R3,V4
(FL-4) Give-Away, **PARISIAN STEAM LAUNDRY**, about 1900, L 11/16", R4, V7
(RL-1) Cast, about 1900, L 2 1/8", R1, V3   **(RL-2)** Cast, like **(RL-1)**, L 1 3/4", R1, V3
(RL-3) Cast, like **(RL-1)**, brass, L 1 5/8", R3, V6
(RL-4) Cast, English, about 1900, L 1 7/8", R2, V5

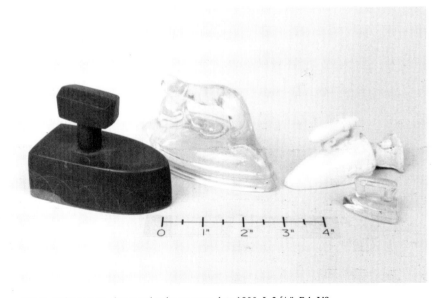

480 (L-1) Soapstone, decorated red soapstone, late 1800, L 3 5/8", R4, V9
(L-2) Glass Candy Container, about 1930, L 3 7/8", R1, V4
(L-3) Staffordshire, English, with baby in blanket for slug, late 1800, L 2 1/2", R5, V9
(L-4) Sandwich Glass, clear glass, late 1800, L 1 3/8", R4, V8

IRON HEATING DEVICES

The devices used to heat irons are as ingenious and as novel as the irons they heated. One common type of iron heater is the stove top style. A stove lid could be lifted out and the iron heater placed over the hole. Other styles were just placed on the flat stove surface. Some stove top models were an open type where the irons were exposed and they heated slowly. Other models had hinged and mechanical coverings to improve heating rates. Another type of heater was the self contained coal/wood burning laundry stove. Such stoves were similar to a typical pot belly stove, but the belly was designed with 6 to 10 flat surfaces around the circumference to heat many irons at the same time. Natural gas heaters are also unique and, like the stove top units, have covers as well as special closures and features.

Collector Hints

Heaters, in general, are unique and interesting to collect. Recently they have become very difficult to find. Look for dated, patented and maker named models. The more decorative and mechanical, the better. No reproductions are known.

481 (L) Laundry Stove, **TIP TOP LAUNDRY, SOUTHERN STOVE WORKS INC, RICHMOND VA, No. 112**, flat sides flare out at top, 8 irons held by a notched clip, rectangular top with 2 stove lids, late 1800, Ht 25", R4, V10
(R) Laundry Stove, **JANES 5 TRADEMARK, JANES & KIRKLAND, NY**, oval top with 2 lids, holds 10 irons on ledge with clips, late 1800, Ht 29 1/2", R4, V10

482 (L) Laundry Stove, **ABC A-4**, holds 10 irons on ledge with teeth, rectangular top with 1 stove lid, late 1800, Ht 26 3/4", R4, V10
(R) Laundry Stove, **MILOR IRON HEAT**, tall and slender stove for tailor's irons, holds 8 irons on ledge with teeth, late 1800, Ht 35 1/2", R5, V11

483 (L) Laundry Stove, **QUAKER BUCKWALTERS STOVE CO, ROYERSFORD PA, No. 98**, holds 10 irons on a ledge, rectangular top with 2 stove lids, late 1800, Ht 25 ½", R4, V10

(R) Laundry Stove, **WALKER & PRATT MFG CO, BOSTON, No. 1**, holds 8 irons on a ledge, oval top with 2 stove lids, late 1800, Ht 28 ½", R4, V10

484 (L) Laundry Stove, **UNION STOVE WORKS, UNION**, holds 6 irons, round top with 1 stove lid, late 1800, Ht 19 ¾", R4, V10

(R) Laundry Stove, **BAESTON STOVE CO, PROV. RI, PATENT APPLIED FOR**, holds 6 irons, round top with 1 stove lid, late 1800, Ht 19 ¾", R4, V10 (Carson)

485 (L) Laundry Stove, **PRIZE #15**, holds 9 irons, oval top with 2 stove lids, late 1800, Ht 27", R4, V10

(R) Laundry Stove, **THE KEELEY STOVE CO, COLUMBIA PA, LAUNDRY IMPROVED, 1900, 8-19**, holds 9 irons, oval top with 2 stove lids, late 1800, Ht 23 ½", R4, V10

486 (L) Laundry Stove, **THE WEHRLE, NEWARK OHIO, No. 38, UTILITY**, holds 8 irons, rectangular top with 4 stove lids, late 1800, Ht 24", R4, V10

(R) Laundry Stove, **BIRMINGHAM BELLE 85, BS & R CO**, holds 8 irons, oval top with 2 stove lids, late 1800, Ht 23 ½", R4, V10

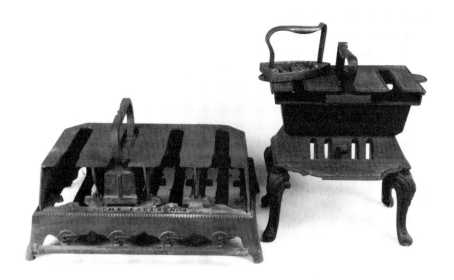

487 (L) Natural Gas, **THE EAGLE, No. 4**, special heater for large (20 lb) tailor's irons, holds 4 irons, late 1800, L 19", R4, V8
(R) Charcoal, French, holds 3 French irons, mid 1800, Ht 14 1/2", R5, V10

488 (L) Natural Gas, European, **PD**, heater for irons with "L" style handles, late 1800, L 14", R3, V7
(M) Natural Gas Heating Stand, heated 1 iron while holding another, early 1900, Ht 7", R3, V6
(R) Natural Gas, **QKL CO, NY**, heater for Mahony style polishers, late 1800, L 10", R3, V7

489 (L) Natural Gas, European, heater for open back ox tongue iron, early 1900, Ht 10", R4, V8 (Holtzman)
(F) Natural Gas, **THE GOODWIN GAS STOVE METER CO, PHILA, CHICAGO, NY**, early 1900, L 11", R4, V8 (Holtzman)
(B) Electric, English, **DOWSINGS HEATER, PAT #515593**, electric iron slides in and couples to the electrodes, early 1900, L 18", R5, V11 (Holtzman)

490 (L) Stove Top, **THE SUN, PAT JULY 5 1881**, holds 2 irons but has 1 gate, L 7 1/2", R5, V9 (Holtzman)
(R) Natural Gas, **EC #12**, holds 4 irons, early 1900, L 18 1/2", R3, V7 (Holtzman)

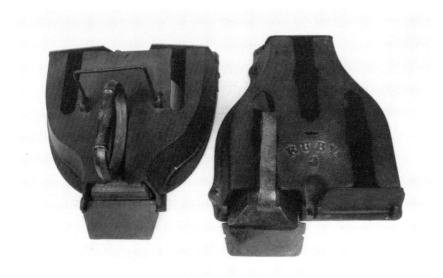

491 **(L)** Stove Top, holds 3 irons, late 1800, L 11", R4, V9
(R) Stove Top, **RUBY 3**, holds 3 irons, late 1800, L 12", R4, V9

492 **(L)** Stove Top, **1884**, holds 2 irons, L 9 ¹/₂", R5, V9
(M) Stove Top or Gas Burner, holds 1 iron, late 1800, L 7 ¹/₂", R3, V6
(R) Stove Top, **PAT MONITOR M**, holds 2 irons, late 1800, L 8", R3, V8

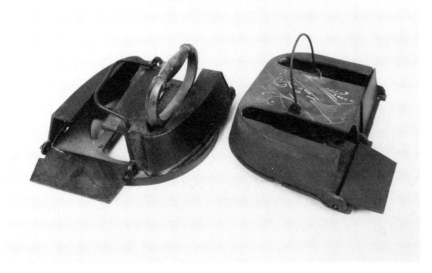

493 **(L)** Stove Top, holds 2 irons, late 1800, L 9", R2, V7
(R) Stove Top, decorated between wire handle, holds 2 irons, late 1800, L 8", R4, V8

494 **(L)** Stove Top, **J.F. RATHBONE & CO, ALBANY NY, J.S. BROOKS PATENT NOV 25 1862, No. 9,** Rochester, NY, holds 3 irons, lift lid, L 24", R5, V10
(R) Stove Top, **CENTENNIAL HEATER, PAT AL'D FEB 1876,** heater sits in stove hole, lid is mechanical and clamps around iron handle posts, L 14", R4, V10

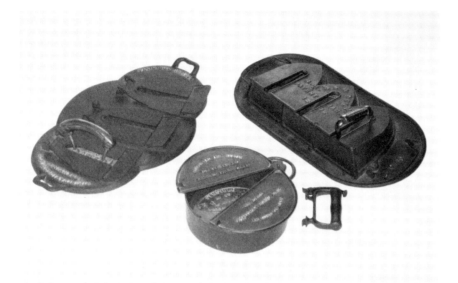

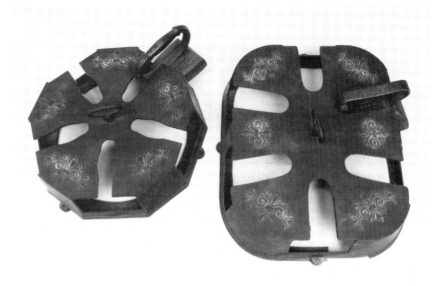

495 (L) Stove Top, **J.M.B. DAVIDSON & CO, ALBANY NY, PAT'D OCT 18 1864**, mechanical, pressure from pushing down on iron raises the slotted lid, L 22 ¾", R5, V11
(M) Stove Top, **NOXALL SAD IRON HEATER, FOR HEATING AND KEEPING IRONS CLEAN, MFG BY QUINCY FOUNDRY & NOVELTY CO, QUINCY ILL**, late 1800, Dia 9 ¼", R5, V10
(R) Stove Top, **R.M. MERRILLS, PATENT JAN 11 1876, No 9**, irons push lever bar to close gates, L 21 ½", R5, V11
(All Herrick)

496 (L) Stove Top, decorated top, holds 5 irons, late 1800, L 13", R5, V10
(R) Stove Top, decorated top like **(L)**, holds 6 irons, late 1800, L 17", R5, V10

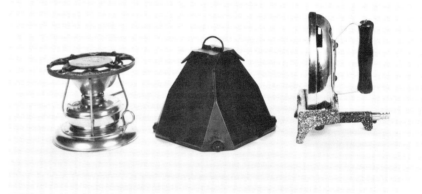

497 (L) Stove Top, **A & W MFG CO, CHICAGO, No. 2, SAD IRON HEATER, PAT'D FEB 13 '83**, plate holds 2 irons, L 8 ½", R3, V7 (Balestri)
(M) Stove Top, **513**, holds 1 iron, late 1800, L 8 ¼", R4, V8 (Balestri)
(R) Stove Top, **A & W MFG CO, CHICAGO, PAT'D FEB 13 '83, No. 3, SAD IRON HEATER**, plate holds 3 irons, L 11 ¾", R3, V7 (Balestri)

498 (L) Alcohol, **UNIVERSAL ALCOHOL STOVE CO, LANDERS, FRARY & CLARK, NEW BRITAIN CONN USA, PATENTED SEPT 8 1908**, Ht 5 ½", R3, V7
(M) Stove Top, **MRS SUSAN R KNOX REVOLVING SAD IRON HEATER, PAT APPL'D FOR**, holds 4 irons, has 4 wheels to rotate heater, late 1800, Ht 6", R5, V11
(R) Natural Gas, French, **LE FER, CC AUG 12, A CHAUFFAGE INTERIEUR**, about 1900, iron L 6 ½", R3, V7
(All Balestri)

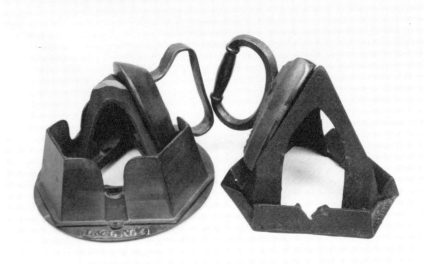

499 (L) Stove Top, pyramid, **S & T CO, CLEV O**, holds 4 irons, late 1800, Ht 8 ½", R5, V10
(R) Stove Top, pyramid, **NORTH'S VENT'D SAD IRON HEATER, PATENT PEND'G**, by W.C. North, vent holes under hood, holds 4 irons, about 1890, Ht 7 ¾", R5, V10

500 (L) Stove Top, **L & L NY**, holds 3 irons, pyramid in center, outer shell holds handle, late 1800, Ht 6", R5, V11
(R) Stove Top, pyramid, holds 3 irons, late 1800, Ht 7", R2, V8

501 (L) Stove Top, pyramid heater cover, sheet metal, holds 3 irons, mid 1800, Ht 6 ¾", R3, V8
(M) Pyramid Iron Heater Center for Heater **(L)**
(R) Charcoal Heating Pot, **MF POTTER, PATENTED JAN 22 1850**, holds 6 irons with a wire, irons point down, Ht 9", R5, V11

502 (FL) Sultana Toilet Iron *[see photo 355]* (Balestri)
(FM) Rotary Hat Iron *[see photo 232]* (Balestri)
(FR) Two Chalfant Irons *[see photo 441]* (Balestri)
(R) Gas Jet, brass fixture for heating hollow body irons, arms movable at joint, late 1800, L 9", R5, V9 (Balestri)

MISCELLANEOUS ITEMS RELATED TO PRESSING IRONS

Collector Hints

All the odd materials that picture irons, look themselves like irons or were used in the ironing process are included in the miscellaneous category. This section includes advertising items, give-aways, pin cushions, special waxing devices, handle grips, removable base plates (shoes), puffing boards, sleeve puffers, and any other materials that were not placed in an earlier category.

Anything related to ironing is collectible today, even trinkets and plastic salt and pepper shakers. Some advertising materials may also be desirable to a group that collects advertising. Other ironing subjects have a similar cross-over market and can be equally desirable - examples are shaving mugs, prints and paintings and give-away items. Specific collecting interest will vary widely for the miscellaneous ironing materials.

503 (FL) Give-Away, **AMERICAN MACHINE CO, PHILADELPHIA, (crown)**, 1876 Centennial piece, handle lifts off like the full size iron, nickel plated over brass, L $^7/_8$", R5, V11
(FM) Give-Away, **ENTERPRISE MFG CO, PHILADA**, like **(FL)**, L $^7/_8$", R4, V10
(FR) Give-Away, side view of **(FL)** and **(FM)**
(R) Toy Set, washboard, iron and wringer, nickel plated, about 1930, Iron L 1 $^1/_8$", R5, V9

504 HOTPOINT, SUPER IRON, original art for advertising, paper water color, about 1920, Ht 19", R5, V11

505 (L) Give-Away, English, **THOMAS OGILVIE & SON**, late 1800, L 3 ³/₄", R4, V9 (Holtzman)
(R) Give-Away, **WH LENT TAILOR SUPPLIES, 682 23rd ST, NEW YORK**, Chinaman in robe, late 1800, L 3 ³/₄", R4, V10

506 (L) Bosom Board, **GEO. W. HARRIS, PAT DEC 15th '74, LOWELL, MASS**, all wood with fabric cover, paper label on back, L 23 ¹/₂", R3, V7
(R) Ruffle Press, all wood with threaded press mechanism, to put large ruffles in fabric, late 1800, L 20", R5, V9

507 (L) Combination, embossing iron patent model, pat. by Frederick Myers, March 11, 1873, pat. #136,613, sad and embossing iron with detachable embossing plates, L 6 ¹/₈", R5, V12 (Walker)
(R) Sad Iron Model, pat. by P.W. Weida, Aug 22, 1871, pat. #118,311, L 6 ¹/₈", R4, V10 (Walker)

508 (L) Heater Patent Model, **S.B. DINSMORE, RICHMOND MAINE**, pat. April 3, 1877, pat. #189,198, miniature version with 2 small irons, L 4 ⁵/₈", R5, V12 (Walker)
(R) Heater Patent Model, pat. Aug 14, 1877 by J.B. Woolsey, pat. #194,284, L 12", R5, V12 (Walker)

509 (L) Clock, **IRONRITE - THE WORLD'S FINEST IRONER**, neon clock, mangle for No. 12, about 1940, Ht 18", R5, V11 (Balestri)
(R) Display, **GENERAL ELECTRIC - THE APPLIANCE MOST WOMEN WANT MOST**, when operating iron moves around the surface, about 1940, Iron L 9", R5, V11 (Balestri)

510 (L-1) Give-Away, **REID BROTHERS - AT THE SIGN OF THE RED GOOSE**, painted red, base is hollow, early 1900, L 3 1/8", R4, V8
(L-2) Give-Away, **J.A. GRIFFITH & CO, BALTIMORE**, some blue paint, early 1900, L 3 1/2", R4, V9
(L-3) Give-Away, **JOS. M . HAYES WOOLEN CO, ST LOUIS**, early 1900, L 3 1/2", R4, V9
(L-4) Give-Away, **JOS. M. HAYES WOOLEN CO, FINE TAILORS TRIMMINGS, ST LOUIS**, early 1900, L 3 3/4", R4, V9 (All Balestri)

511 (FL) Pin Cushion, **EB**, painted wood, about 1875, L 6 1/4", R3, V7
(FR) Pin Cushion, stencil decoration, about 1875, L 6 1/2", R4, V8
(R) Sewing Box, all wood with metal heat shield, rear hinge for top, late 1800, L 7 1/4", R5, V11

512 (L) Suitcase Iron, **IRO-CASE, JANIS INC**, handle of suitcase is electric iron, about 1930, L 21 1/4", R5, V11
(R) Electric Mangle, **GENERAL ELECTRIC**, about 1940, L 22", R2, V4

513 (FL) Cold Handle, wood grip for sad iron, about 1900, L 6 1/4", R3, V4 (Carson)
(FR) Cold Handle, **PAT MAR 5 '98**, L 5 1/4", R2, V2
(RL) Cold Handle, **ENTERPRISE, REGISTERED IN US PATENT OFFICE**, early 1900, L 5 3/4", R3, V4
(RM) Cold Handle and Iron Stand, early 1900, L 5 3/4", R2, V3
(RR) Cold Handle, **PAT APL'D FOR**, about 1900, L 5 1/2", R2, V3

514 (FL) Trivet, European, chip carved decoration, early 1800, L 7 3/4", R5, V9
(FR) Fabric Print, European, copper feather pattern on bottom to imprint fabric, late 1800, L 6 1/4", R4, V8
(RL) Iron Sole Plate, about 1900, L 7", R3, V4
(RM) Iron Sole Plate, pat. by Charles Burk, Chicago, 1910, L 6 1/4", R3, V4
(RR) Iron Sole Plate, about 1920, L 6 3/4", R3, V4

515 (FL) Waxer, **GRAND MA'S PERFUMED WAXING PAD, COLUMBIA WAX WORKS**, about 1900, Ht 7 3/8", R5, V5
(FM) Waxer, **SUPER PERFUMED IRONING WAX PAD**, about 1900, Ht 6 1/2", R4, V4
(FR) Advertising, **ELASTIC STARCH, JC HUBINGER BROS, CONN**, 1910, Ht 6", R2, V3
(RL) Waxers, wood knob, Ht 2 1/4", R2, V3
(RM) Polish, **IRON-DANDY POLISH**, C.H. Rath Co, Phila PA, about 1900, Ht 3 3/4", R4, V4
(RR) Waxer, **THE IDEAL FLAT IRON CLEANER, PATENTED APRIL 13 1897**, The Bodine Roofing Co, L 5", R4, V4

516 (FL) Trade Card, **ENTERPRISE MFG CO**, about 1900, L 4 1/2", R2, V2
(FR) Trade Card, **MRS POTTS SAD IRON**, about 1900, L 4 3/4", R2, V2
(RL) Trade Card, **MRS FLORENCE POTTS**, about 1900, Ht 4 1/2", R2, V2
(RM) Trade Card, **CONQUEROR WRINGER**, about 1900, L 5", R2, V2
(RR) Trade Card, **GENEVA HAND FLUTER**, late 1800, Ht 3 3/4", R2, V2

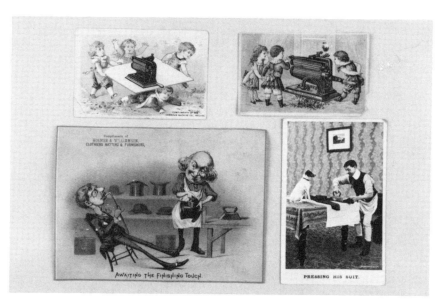

517 **(FL)** Trade Card, **HOSMER & WILLIAMSON, CLOTHIERS, HATTERS AND FURNISHERS**, late 1800, L 7", R3, V4
(FR) Post Card, England, about 1900, Ht 5 1/2", R2, V3
(RL) Trade Card, **THE AMERICAN MACHINE CO**, late 1800, L 4 3/8", R2, V2
(RR) Trade Card, like **(RL)**, L 4 1/4", R2, V2

518 **(FL)** Trade Card, **CASCADE STEAM LAUNDRY, GREAT FALL NH**, about 1900, L 5 1/2", R2, V2
(FR) Trade Card, **AMERICAN MACHINE CO, PHILA PA**, late 1800, L 4 1/2", R2, V2
(M) Post Card, German, about 1900, Ht 5 3/8", R1, V1
(RL) Trade Card, **THE AMERICAN MACHINE CO**, about 1900, L 5", R2, V2
(RR) Trade Card, like **(RL)**, L 4 1/2", R2, V2

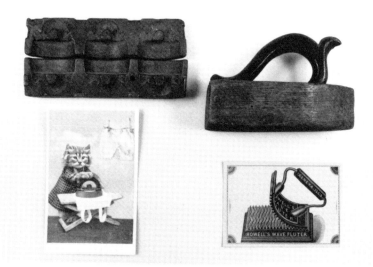

519 **(FL)** Post Card, Switzerland, about 1920, Ht 5 1/2", R3, V2 (Eubanks)
(FR) Trade Card, **HOWELL'S WAVE FLUTER**, late 1800, L 4 1/2", R5, V6 (Eubanks)
(RL) Candy Mold, cast iron, French cap iron style, early 1900, L 6 1/4", R5, V6 (Eubanks)
(RR) Wood Smoother, all wood polisher, late 1800, L 5 1/2", R4, V7

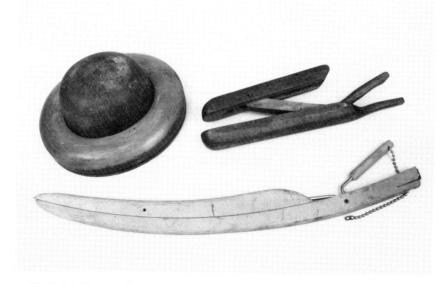

520 **(F)** Suit Sleeve Puffer, all wood, expands when 2 handles are squeezed, about 1900, L 31", R3, V4
(RL) Hat Form, all wood, 2 pieces, late 1800, L 15", R1, V2
(RR) Sleeve Puffer, all wood, expands like **(F)**, about 1900, L 19", R3, V4

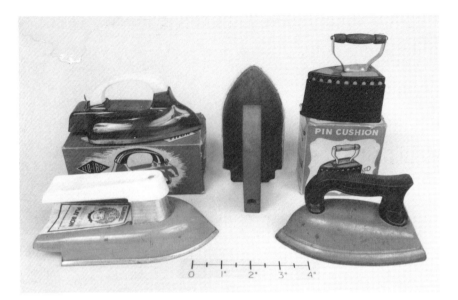

521 (L) Pleater, **THE NEW VICTORIA PLEATER, PRICE $2.⁰⁰, PATENTED 1905**, tin with paper label, L 13 ¹/₂", R1, V3
(M) Pleater, pat. Feb 22, 1876 by Anderson and Rorke, wood frame, L 12 ¹/₂", R2, V6
(R) Pleater, **CHAMPION LIGHTNING NEEDLE PLAITER**, tin with needles, early 1900, L 11 ³/₄", R2, V4

522 (FL) **RAGGEDY ANN PLAY IRON**, tin/plastic, 1970, L 5 ³/₈", R2, V3
(FR) Toy, electric, tin/plastic, 1950, L 5 ¹/₄", R1, V2
(RL) **GLO IRON**, red clear plastic, orig box, mid 1900, L 4 ⁵/₈", R2, V4
(RM) Porcelain, about 1935, L 4 ¹/₂", R2, V4
(RR) Pin Cushion with Tape Measure, orig box, 1967, L 3", R1, V2

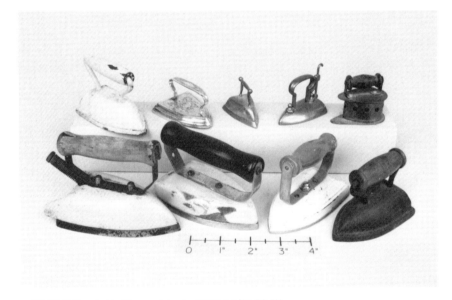

523 (FL-1) Give-Away, **FENSTERMAKER, LANCASTER PA**, brass ashtray, about 1920, L 3", R2, V6
(FL-2) Give-Away, **SAFERON- MASSENGILL**, about 1940, L 3 ¹/₈", R2, V4
(FL-3) Give-Away, **STUART FOR IRON DEFICIENCY ANEMIA**, mid 1900, L 3 ³/₄", R2, V4
(FL-4) Give-Away, **FOLK'S FESCHT 1941, LENCESCHTER CO**, L 2 ³/₈", R1, V4
(FL-5) Give-Away, **NORCO FOUNDRY, POTTSTOWN PA**, mid 1900, L 3", R1, V4
(RL) Decorative, brass, mid 1900, L 5 ¹/₂", R2, V4
(RM) Give-Away, **LEHMAN HARDWARE, KIDRON OH**, mid 1900, L 3 ⁵/₈", R2, V5 (Carson)
(RR) Decorative, brass, mid 1900, L 4 ¹/₂", R2, V4

524 (FL-1) Toy, electric, blue porcelain, about 1925, L 4 ¹/₈", R2, V4
(FL-2) Toy, electric, English, **REP LIMITED**, blue porcelain, about 1930, L 3 ⁷/₈", R2, V4
(FL-3) Toy, tin, about 1930, L 3 ⁵/₈", R2, V3   **(FL-4)** Toy, about 1920, L 3 ³/₈", R2, V3
(RL-1) Toy, like **(FL-4)**, L 3 ³/₈", R2, V3
(RL-2) Toy, Mexican, engraved, about 1940, L 2 ¹/₂", R3, V4 (Carson)
(RL-3) Toy, brass, about 1950, L 2", R1, V2   **(RL-4)** Toy, brass, about 1970, L 2 ¹/₈", R1, V2 (Carson)
(RL-5) Toy, brass, about 1960, L 2 ¹/₄", R1, V2

DISCLAIMER

This book should be used only as a general reference guide and not as a definitive value source. I have listed value information based upon my thoughts at the time of publication, relative to my interest and regional demands. The author shall not be held liable and/or responsible for damages of any nature, caused or alleged to be caused, directly or indirectly by information or statements contained in this book.

REFERENCES

1. Berney, Esther S., *A Collector's Guide to Pressing Irons and Trivets*, Crown Publisher, NY (1977).
2. Glissman, A. H., *The Evolution of the Sad Iron*, Carlsbad, CA (1970).
3. Irons, Dave, *Pressing Iron Patents*, Northampton, PA (1994).
4. Jewel, Brian, *Smoothing Irons*, Wallace-Homestead Book Company, Des Moines, IA (1977).
5. Politzer, Judy, *Early Tuesday Morning*, Walnut Creek, CA (1986).
6. Politzer, Judy, *Tuesday's Children*, Walnut Creek, CA (1977).
7. St. John, Oliver, *Gallimaufry of Goffering*, Cobham Surrey, England (1982).
8. Swanson, Vi, *Sad-Irons and their Trademarks*, Seattle, WA (1984).

INDEX

160